The New Age of Soul

Spiritual Wisdom for a New Millennium

Ray S. Anderson

Wipf and Stock Publishers
150 West Broadway ♦ Eugene OR 97401

Wipf and Stock Publishers
150 West Broadway
Eugene, Oregon 97401

The New Age of Soul
Spiritual Wisdom for a New Millennium
By Anderson, Ray S.
©2001 Anderson, Ray S.
ISBN: 1-57910-815-6
Publication Date: November, 2001

Revised layout January, 2002.

The New Age of Soul

Spiritual Wisdom for a New Millennium

Ray S. Anderson
4015 Humboldt Drive
Huntington Beach, CA 92649
November 2001

Contents

Preface	7
1. Introduction: The Loss of Soul	9
2. The New Age of Soul: Evolving Toward Divinity	17
3. The Divine Imprint of Soul: Bearing The Birthmarks of Humanity	33
4. The Community of Soul: No One is an Island	45
5. The Redemption of the Soul: Whatever Became of Sin?	53
6. The Spiritual Nature of the Soul: Living with Faith, Hope and Love	63
7. The Companion of the Soul: Creative Partnering With God	77
8. The Healing of the Soul: Recovering From Deep Injuries to the Soul	89
9. The Care of the Soul: A Guide to Spiritual Fitness	115
10. The Resurrection of the Soul: A Vision of Life Beyond Death	87
Bibliography	127
Endnotes	134

Preface

It may be no accident that, simultaneous with the search for physical life forms in outer space through modern technology guided by physicists with mystical vision, the end of the second millennium and the beginning of a new one finds the human spirit on a quest for a spiritual life form within the inner space of the self. When new age spirituality finds a soul mate in the mystical musings of contemporary physics, we may be experiencing the dawn of a new millennium. Mysticism and spirituality are twins separated at birth by the forceps of modern technology without a soul. Welcome to the family!

I could move the world, the Greek philosopher and mathematician Archimedes was reported to have said, given a lever of sufficient length and a place on which to rest it. Driven by unrelenting curiosity and seduced by sophisticated technology, the human spirit has stepped off one planet onto another. The world has moved.

What was ruled out as esoteric and unthinkable by the rational skepticism of post-enlightenment scientists who worshipped at the shrine of objectivity, has become subjectively undeniable by their children. It was not a theologian but a physicist, who unlocked the mystery of the atom and paused at the threshold of the immensity of this new world of reality to bow in worship and give a nod to a Creator. It was not because Einstein was by religious heritage a Jew that he found a place for God and a spiritual perception of reality; rather he was compelled, as a subject drawn into the objective reality of creation itself, to acknowledge the gift of soul as the coefficient of all true knowledge.

Spiritual wisdom is a matter of the soul, and where soul is diminished, knowledge may increase but folly prevail. We enter the new millennium as spiritual beings who are also human. Our concern for spirituality can become an obsession which leads to delusion. That would be folly. It is spiritual wisdom that we seek, not merely spiritual experience. "I was ambushed by spirituality," wrote one contemporary seeker. Seeking relief from the relentless barrenness of life without spirit, he sought comfort in meditation, only to discover God. "I used to think the soul was a metaphor. Now I know there is a God—my God, in here, demanding not faith but experience, an inexhaustible wonder at the richness of this very moment."[1]

As a practical theologian and pastoral caregiver, I deal with what medieval theologians quaintly called, "the cure of souls." I have a concern for the soul, not as an entity or object of philosophical thought and scientific investigation, but as the quality of life that marks humans off from all other non-human species, which bonds persons one to another, and which is the source of a spiritual life which reflects the image and likeness of God. This is not just another book about the new age movement, or about new age spirituality as such. It is a book about the human soul, and an attempt to redefine the soul from the perspective of a Judeo-Christian tradition and in the context of a new age spirituality which has colored the soul with its own hue of mystical, transcendental psychology. My purpose is to outline the contours of a spiritual wisdom that will guide and empower us for an authentic and liberating life of faith for a new millennium.

I hope to reveal the soul not as an alien resident among us, but as that which makes us most human because it is out of the soul that we discover our own authentic spiritual nature and the one true God in whose image we were created. With the advent of the third millennium since the birth of Jesus, it is again time to take stock of our souls, as the English playwright, Christopher Fry reminds us:

> "Affairs are now soul size. The enterprise
> is exploration into God"[2]

ONE

Introduction: *The Loss of Soul*

When soul is neglected, it doesn't just go away; it appears symptomatically in obsessions, addictions, violence, and loss of meaning... the root problem is that we have lost our wisdom about the soul, even our interest in it. (Thomas Moore)[3]

    The surfeit of stimulation to the senses in our media driven culture would appear to satisfy the most ravenous hunger. What is not constantly available in the public arena is instantly accessible through the cyberspace of internet. How much pornography must be consumed before the appetite for it is quenched? We would have expected that the human soul finally had its fill of the obscene and the depraved. It does not work that way. We no longer have confidence that what outrages our senses would stir us toward sensibility. There only remains a deep and disquieting sadness that surely, at least, must be the echo of a Divine sigh.
    Were we not once optimistic that the insanity of violence would itself make humanity more sane in its respect for the dignity and value of life? How much more violence disseminated as 'breaking news' is needed to dull the appetite for the 'close up' shots of bleeding bodies, terror stricken faces, and inconsolable weeping? Perhaps we once had confidence that the surrogate violence of

video games would inoculate our children against the real thing. Murderous impulses can be safely discharged through vicarious participation in harmless graphic images on the big screen or computer monitor—did not some of our social scientists assure us of that? Now we see that the line between virtual reality and reality itself tends to be erased by the constant rubbing of images against imagination.

When children commit violence against other children, the line between fantasy and reality has been crossed. The two boys in Colorado who shot their classmates in cold blood had 'killed' hundreds if not thousands of humanlike figures on their computer games before moving into their High School with real bullets. One wonders if they were stunned to realize that there was no way to push a button to 'save this game,' and play it another day. Reality is unforgiving. Instant replay only occurs on television.

This descent into the abyss of human aberration has not gone unnoticed and unreported, more openly by the secular commentators than by religious prophets. We have always had the prophets of doom. They are still there, on the sidelines, raising their placards and chanting their slogans. But we are seeking analysis and perspective, not denunciation and warning. So we turn to those euphemistically called 'anchor persons' for clues, only to find them without anchor and without a clue. The wisdom of the pundits becomes a chorus of shrill magpies; 'talking heads' lament and lambaste, pontificate and pronounce, with a tacit agreement never to come to consensus.

In the midst of the crosscurrents of blaming and excusing, explaining and complaining, voices can be heard pointing to the loss of something vital to the essence of humanity itself. It goes far deeper than the crisp and clinical critique in T. S. Elliott's classic elegy, "The Hollow Men." We are talking about a moral and spiritual abyss, not contentless cardboard figures masquerading as real people. It goes deeper yet than the more recent unmasking of the 'shades of mediocrity' in the haunting lyrics of Simon and Garfunkel. Nor will a 'bridge over troubled waters' carry us across this abyss of inhumanity, for the underpinning of humanity itself appears to have disappeared.

Thomas Moore, I think, got it right when he said, "The great malady of the twentieth century, implicated in all of our troubles and affecting us individually and socially, is 'loss of soul.'" When we neglect the soul, Moore went on to say, "it doesn't just go away; it appears symptomatically in obsessions, addictions, violence, and loss of meaning. Our temptation is to isolate these symptoms or to try to eradicate them one by one; but the root problem is that we have lost our wisdom about the soul, even our interest in it."[4]

Lamenting the loss of a concept of a human soul among secular psychiatrists, M. Scott Peck writes, "why is it that the word 'soul' is not in the professional lexicon of psychiatrists, other mental health works, students of the mind, and physicians in general?" His conclusion is that because 'God talk' is inherent in the concept of the soul, and 'God talk' is virtually off-limits in the secular mental profession, the soul has been ignored.[5]

What ever has happened to the soul?

Have we lost the semantic connection between the word and the experience itself? If so, then we are more than at a loss for a word, for something that still remains as an essential core of the human person. Whatever we once meant by a soul, it is still there, but we can no longer define it or discuss it. Or, have we lost something of the soul itself? In our neglect of it have we caused it to reappear in a more insidious and tormented form?

How do I explain what loss of soul means? It means the loss of some essential connectedness of persons, to their own inner core of selfhood, to other persons as 'soul mates,' and to God as the source of our personal and spiritual existence. I think of the soul, not as a substance contained within the body, but as the inner core of the whole person, including the body. By 'soul' I mean the personal and spiritual dimension of the self. Thus, the phrase 'body and soul' is not intended to suggest that the soul is something which is merely 'in' the body, or separate from the body, but the whole person with both an interior and an exterior life in the world.

I like Ernest Becker's analysis of the neurotic and obsessive tendencies of our contemporary culture. Becker reminds us that we once lived most of our life within smaller, more cohesive communities. These communities, such as the rural village in middle America where I was raised, provided 'ready made' rituals by which each person in the community could find a meaningful place to rest their souls, when taken by tragedy, grief, suffering, as well as in the celebrations of the mystery of birth and life. In being separated from these communities through our modern, urban, isolated, and anonymous life style, we are forced to contrive and invent rituals to satisfy the needs of our souls personally and privately. In Becker's analysis, this accounts for neurotic obsession with private ritualistic patterns which seek to relieve anxiety and mask our dread of the unknown and unpredictable. While Moore points correctly to the effects of loss of soul in the symptoms of obsessions and addictions, Becker uncovers the deeper source of this loss of soul in being disconnected from the ethos and social structures that provide the rituals and mythical elements that house our souls.[6]

When our souls shrink in the face of the demands of life and the certainty of our mortality, Becker suggests that we seek 'larger souls,' heroic figures, upon which we can project our own identity. We thus seek to 'immortalize' ourselves by transference of self identify, or what I call soul, to something larger than life, something that carries a larger soul, even though it is also the bearer of suffering and tragedy.

What else explains the fascination and preoccupation with the life and then the death of the late Princess Diana? For North Americans, it was not so much that she was part of a *royal* family but that she was part of a royal *family*. The deep grief and display of public mourning displayed around the world reflected the way in which people felt connected to her. Even in death, she became a more beautiful soul than in real life.

More recently, the tragic death of John F. Kennedy, Jr., the son of the former President Kennedy, along with his wife and her sister in a plane crash, brought forth similar manifestations of grief that cut across all other political, social and sectarian lines. "Why do some people grieve more deeply for this man than for their own relatives," a T. V. commentator asked? The answer, of course, is that grief is relative to the loss experienced by the soul. And when the soul is connected by adulation and admiration to another soul that is "larger than life," and more beautiful in death than in life, the grief is greater. We grieve most deeply for our gods when they die, for they are the extension of our souls. When grief becomes heroic it connects our fragmentary and fragile lives to a commonality of soul, a surrogate family of the soul, as it were.

Without some understanding of the soul, we cannot fathom the depths of our depravity, the delirium of our obsessions, nor the delights of our imaginations. Nor can we clarify and conform our most profound spiritual aspirations, without a sense of the soul.

Moore has correctly pointed to the symptoms of loss of soul in the compulsive and obsessive violence that plagues our people. I believe this loss of soul to be a loss of the connection of our individual souls to the fundamental and core structure of soul itself as embodied in the communities that provide a place for our souls to expand without becoming inhuman and grotesque.

If humans are endowed with a uniqueness which includes, moral, spiritual and social capacity, alongside of a rational mind, and if we call this 'soul,' then even the most evil and depraved person is still human—that is has soul. And it is precisely this 'soul' that makes humans more dangerous and destructive than animals, who can only be 'beastly' by virtue of their nature as beasts, while humans can become virtually inhuman by virtue of their nature as humans.

I was recently bitten on the leg by a dog who came upon me from behind as I was walking past a neighbor's house. The dog was neither 'mad' nor 'rabid;' it was only 'being a dog.' I do not attribute the quality of having a 'soul' to a dog in the same sense as I do to a human person. When dogs become deranged we attribute it to a disease. Some dogs by nature have instincts toward fighting and biting. We ought to know the difference between the nature or temperament of dogs when we have them as pets as distinguished from using them for hunting or as guard dogs. When a dog becomes rabid we dispose of the dog rather than treating it as a 'problem of the soul.'

With humans, however, while we allow for different temperaments and dispositions, we hold them accountable to have and express their 'souls' in relationship. The owner of the dog who injured me was contrite, compassionate toward me, and accepted responsibility for the actions of the dog. If he had failed to respond in this way, I would not have excused it as part of his nature, as I did his dog, but a problem of the soul.

Concern for the 'soul' as expressed by Thomas Moore does not necessitate a view of the soul as a separate mental or spiritual entity alongside or within the body. Rather, concern for the soul is concern for the quality of human life at the deepest core of our existential life, at the center of the ecology of our physical life as life in the cosmos, in the manifestation of the divine image in our manifold social relations, and as the spiritual beings that we are by the breath of God's Spirit.

According to best selling author Gary Zukav, humans are evolving from a five-sensory existence into multi-sensory persons. The life of the soul possesses a kind of 'sixth sense' which enables us to tap into the invisible, divine 'intelligence' which frees us from the tyranny of fearful and violent emotions.[7] Love, compassion and wisdom, says Zukav, do not come from the personality but are experiences of the soul. Keith Miller describes the soul as "that most central and mysterious spiritual consciousness [which] operates as a guide to all kinds of everyday human reality, to self-esteem, and to God."[8]

This is what I call the 'uncommon sense' of the soul.

I too believe that the soul has a 'sense' which goes beyond the five senses by which we experience our ordinary lives. The uncommon sense of the soul may begin as a form of spiritual hunger that awakens within us to cause unrest, if not uneasiness. We become seekers, unsatisfied with religious dogma but hungry for a spiritual connection with some ultimate meaning. The 'sense of the soul' is a form of spiritual wisdom into which we can tap when life rises up and hits us squarely in the face and renders us senseless.

When Marty Kaplan, former speechwriter for Vice President Walter Mondale and Hollywood studio executive and screenwriter, turned to meditation in quest of inner peace, he reported, "The spirituality of it ambushed me." Crediting his pilgrimage from secularism to belief in God to the mystical power of meditation, he said, "I thought I would spend my life as a cultural Jew, an agnostic, a closet nihilist. Of course I didn't like it. Who wants to face death without God? Who wants to tell kids that the universe is indifferent to them? . . . What attracted me to meditation was its apparent religious neutrality." Kaplan explained, "I used to think of psychic phenomenon as New Age flimflam. I used to think of reincarnation as a myth. I used to think the soul was a metaphor. Now I know there is a God—my God, in here, demanding not faith but experience, an inexhaustible wonder at the richness of this very moment."[9]

Will the dawning of the third millennium cause the sinister shadows of our psychic demons to vanish in the rosy glow of a new age of the soul? If we have failed to find a god in the cosmos, for all of our secular searching, can we discover the divine within our own soul through a new age of spiritual sensing? This is one compelling alternative, and demands a closer look.

TWO

The New Age of Soul: Evolving Toward Divinity

The entire physical universe itself is nothing more than patterns of neuronal energy firing off inside our heads. . . There is no physical world 'out there.' Consciousness creates all. (Michael Talbot)[10]

    The flower children of the 60s no longer stick flowers in the barrels of rifles held by soldiers in the national guard, chanting, 'make love, not war.' Many have grown up to become corporate executives, stock brokers, and free thinking intellectuals on university faculties. The lure of suburban life domesticated the wild and frenzied tribes whose promiscuous passions were fueled by the equally promiscuous blankets of napalm laid on innocent civilians in Vietnam. Being no longer children with no war to protest, they turned their passionate energy for a more humane world into a pursuit of self-fulfillment. The tools of technology suddenly seemed less sinister when tamed and compelled to be servants of self-aggrandizement.
    The dawn of the age of Aquarius with its leisurely promise of sexual freedom has become a frantic and frenzied pursuit of the sensual pleasure offered by electronic wizardry. Once the sun reaches midday, its blazing rays drive away the soft hues of dawn and there is no return. Twilight, and then darkness lie ahead. Speed, efficiency,

compactness urge us to make use of the light while we have it. Once captured by our poets and lifted by our imagination into aesthetic realms, we now expect the computer chip to carry us into the cybernetic realm of virtual reality.

In retrospect, the unguarded optimism that led Harvard theologian Harvey Cox to write his best selling book of the 60s, *The Secular City*, seems more curious than compelling. Twenty years later Cox revised his thesis and published, *Religion in the Secular City: Toward a Postmodern Theology* and, more recently, a book that reflects his awareness of the rise of spirituality rather than its demise, *Fire From Heaven: The Rise of Pentecostal Spirituality and the Reshaping of Religion in the Twenty-First Century*.[11]

The revival of interest in religion and spirituality as represented by Cox, however, is only a concession to a flame that will not die out and a confession that the autonomy of the new 'secular man' who has replaced religion with science is itself a myth.

The so-called New Age Movement is less a clearly defined entity than a moving and pulsating amoeba. John Drane suggests that it may have antecedents going back as far as five hundred years but emerging more visibly and with greater vitality in our post-enlightenment, and postmodern era. "Anything offering the possibility of a change in human outlook is being seized upon with great enthusiasm. Elements from eastern mysticism combine with modern psychoanalysis, meditation techniques and holistic health to produce a complex maze of pathways to personal fulfilment and wholeness."[12] Russell Chandler suggests that New Age is a modern revival of ancient religious traditions, drawing upon first century gnosticism, Eastern mysticism, modern philosophy and psychology, science and science fiction and the counterculture of the '50s and '60s.[13]

More than anything else, the theme of spirituality pervades the movement, ranging from esoteric philosophical mysticism to sensual ecological pantheism. New Age spirituality is a parallel universe with little resemblance to more traditional forms of spirituality. If it has antecedents in certain fringe elements of traditional Christianity, such as first century gnosticism, it has no ancestors in the biblical story. The new age movement has no territorial markers and no ruling authorities. Its extension is global, if not celestial. Its gospel is one of health, healing, spiritual development and higher consciousness.[14]

What was once tolerated as a curious fascination with Eastern Religion with its culture of meditation, asceticism, and transcendental mysticism, has now emerged as a mainstream movement which markets its products in specialty stores and cloaks its philosophy in quasi-Christian concepts. The Indian spiritual healer, Deepak Chopra, a physician (endocrinologist) came to the United States in 1970. While his religious orientation is Hinduism, he is a mystic with a propensity for marketing spirituality as the 'quantum physics' of universal energy of which each person is a component and participant. His book, *Ageless Body, Timeless Mind*, published in 1993, led to a succession of writings selling more than 6 million copies.[15]

From a more traditional perspective, Herbert Benson of Harvard Medical School was among the first medical researchers to link prayer and meditation to physical healing and total well-being. Benson's research revealed not only that prayer produced positive results in physical healing, but also that the form of prayer was irrelevant to its effectiveness.[16] Encouraged by Benson's approach toward combining medical treatment with meditation, relaxation and prayer, the deeper connection between spirituality and neurobiology continues to be explored. David Felton, Chairman of the department of Neurobiology at the University of Rochester, states: "Anything involved with meditation and controlling the state of mind that alters hormone activity has the potential to have an impact on the immune system." Rhawn Joseph, a neuroscientist at the Palto Alto VA Medical Center in California says, "The ability to have religious experiences has a neuro-anatomical basis."[17]

Larry Dossey, while rejecting some of the new age concepts that spiritual attainment is the overcoming of bad karma which causes sickness and disease, nonetheless argues from his own anecdotal experience that the mind, through prayer, can effect healing 'at a distance.' Dossey admits that he cannot explain the connection between the mind, prayer and healing, but he insists that there is evidence that it exists. *"We simply don't know* how the mind of one person can engage in 'action at a distance' to bring about helpful changes in someone else."[18] The fact that such prayer does produce healing is accounted for through Dossey's belief that 'mental energy' does not 'fade away' with increasing distance. He attributes the effects of prayer to the power of the subconscious self.

> We will never be able to take full advantage of the power of the mind to shape our health—including the mind's use of prayer—until we broaden our concept of 'consciousness.' This means including the unconscious and acknowledging that that is more than the hangout of the bogeyman and monster we generally think it to be. If we do so, we shall see that the unconscious can be extraordinarily helpful and benevolent in our quest for health. In fact, *the unconscious mind can initiate or cooperate with prayer and even mediate the effects.* (emphasis in the original)[19]

At the other end of the continuum, the proponents of new age 'higher consciousness' rely on 'spirit guides' to provide counsel and direction ranging from such mundane tasks as shopping to more sophisticated experiences of encountering transcendental mysteries of the universe. Transpersonal psychologist Barry McWaters, in his book *Conscious Evolution*, puts it this way. "We are listening for messages of guidance from every possible source; tuning in our astro-radios, talking to dolphins, and listening more and more attentively to the words of those among us with psychic abilities. Is there help out there? Is there guidance in here? Will anyone respond?"[20]

For some, a more immediate connection with other spiritual entities occurs through 'channeling,' where one's own thoughts and words purport to come as though dictated by the spirit of a person no longer alive. Those who purport to be 'channelers'—often simply called a channel, "go into a trance state to establish contact with a spirit, ascended mater, off-planet being, higher consciousness, or even an evolved human entity. The channel then receives and repeats the messages and impressions from the 'other side.'"[21]

One of the most remarkable of these claims resulted in the publication of a three-volume work, *The Course in Miracles*, consisting of almost 700 pages accompanied by a student handbook and a teacher's manual. New York psychologist Helen Schueman claimed to have received this material while in a trance between 1965 and 1972. The book alleges to contain messages from, among others, Jesus Christ himself.[22]

Belief in some form of reincarnation is an underlying premise of much new age thought. By inducing hypnotic regression, some have claimed to uncover past lives of persons and information otherwise unknown to them, as evidence of reincarnation. Such anecdotal evidence, while not empirically verifiable, is nonetheless compelling for those who find it somehow reassuring to believe that their present existence is a projection of a former one, and that their soul will survive death in yet another form.

For the most part, the spirit entities encountered through channeling appear to be benign and ready to provide the kind of good news that the seeker wishes to hear. An ad for a channeling course puts it well: "Channeling is a powerful and exciting way to discover the higher purpose in your life. Following your higher purpose will bring great gifts of joy, aliveness, and self-love. The ability to connect with a high level guide is a skill that can be learned easily and joyfully. Therefore, the goal of this course is to create a conscious link with your guide so you can channel higher guidance of love and light, thus empowering yourself and others."[23]

On the other hand, some are not so fortunate in their encounter with the spirit world. Robert Monroe, in his book, *Journeys Out of the Body*, reports an out of body experience where he was viciously attacked by what he identified as evil spirits, two of whom changed into images of his daughters in an effort to unbalance him.[24]

While New Age spirituality looks deep into the self in a search for a source of power and meaning as well as a connection to a higher spirit world, there is little mention or concern about the soul. One exception is Elizabeth Clare Prophet. She affirms belief in Jesus Christ and labels herself a Christian, but tends toward the ancient gnostic form of a spiritual cosmology through which the true teachings of Jesus could be found. Key to her version of spirituality is the 'Christ Self,' which is one and the same with Jesus and our own higher consciousness. Below the 'Christ Self,' is what she calls the 'soul self,' the self we live with day to day in our ordinary experiences. The divine I AM extends through Jesus Christ and ends with the soul self in each person. This, she claims, is the spark of divinity that lies within each waiting to be fanned into a brilliant flame.[25]

While 'higher consciousness' once served to differentiate new age thought from more traditional Judeo-Christian spirituality, Gary Zukav uses the concept of 'soul' to create a more positive link. Perhaps it is only a matter of rushing in to fill the void left by the 'loss of soul' described by Thomas Moore. Perhaps it is also the result of the virtual abandonment of the concept of soul in more traditional Christian thought due to embarrassment over the charge of being only concerned with 'saving souls.' His book, *The Seat of the Soul*, continues to be a best seller and receives high acclaim from millions of readers as well as talk show hosts such as Oprah Winfrey. For new age spirituality, Zukav provides his own brand of theological legitimacy by redefining both God and the human self through the concept of soul.

With Zukav, the concept of the soul reaches a new level in the literature of new age spirituality and touches a theological nerve in the core of more traditional Judeo-Christian views of humans as spiritual beings. Many who read his book conclude that he presents a viable and compelling alternative to the older tradition. What millions find so attractive in his teaching compels us to take a closer look at what he says about the soul.

Soul, asserts Zukav, constitutes an inner core of personal being as over and against the personality and physical existence itself. The soul of every person is a smaller piece of Divine Intelligence in the process of becoming itself god.[26] Each soul (person) is a "reduction of an immortal Life system into the framework of time and the span of a few years."[27] Or, to put it more plainly, as he does by illustration, if the ocean were conceived to be the vast, undifferentiated 'soul' of immortal and divine reality, each individual person is like a cup dipped into the ocean which now contains in a limited and small way, what is essentially constituted by the whole.

He believes that the soul cannot exist in a time/space framework apart from a physical body and its attending personality. The personality operates as does the physical body in terms of external power, which is competitive, moralistic, and unforgiving. The soul constitutes the inner or authentic power of the self above and beyond the grasp of personality (psychology) and the mind (rationality). "The personality does not operate independently from the soul. To the extent that a person is in touch with spiritual depths, the personality is soothed because the energy of consciousness is focused on its energy core and not on its artificial façade, which is the personality."[28]

The five senses constitute the limits by which external power operates and thus precludes the self from operating at the level of the soul. Only a 'spiritual psychology,' argues Zukav, operating out of a multisensory capacity can understand and interact with the soul.

The soul is thus not a religious component of the self, but the very core of the self's essential being as unbounded by the external form of the self and its five sensory environment. What are taken to be inappropriate or harmful behaviors and attitudes, are not to be located in the personality, but rather in the soul. Each human soul has had numerous previous existences in some human form, and carries with it karma debts from that existence which must be understood, acknowledged, and changed through conscious choice to move toward a higher state of the soul. The soul does not emerge in a person free of predispositions of both a negative and positive force. To use his analogy, the cup of soul which each of us possess has been used before! But we are responsible to leave it in better shape when we return it. In this way, the soul, when it 'returns home,' to use Zukav's expression, will be in a higher spiritual state than when it was received.

Each person's soul is an incarnation of soul, which has had earlier incarnations. "If your soul was a Roman centurion, an Indian beggar, a Mexican mother, a nomad boy, and a medieval nun, among other incarnations, for example, and if the karmic patterns that were set into motion within those lifetimes are in motion within you, you will not be able to understand your proclivities, or interests, or ways of responding to different situations without an awareness of the experiences of those lifetimes."[29]

Is the soul then human or divine? Both, Zukav would say. Being human is to have an individual soul. Animals do not have an individual soul. There is only one soul for each species. At the same time, Zukav says that human souls have emerged from the 'soul pool' of animals, so to speak, through a process of evolution. The evolutionary leap through which human souls emerged differentiate humans from animals as spiritual beings. That is, humans by virtue of having a soul are now on an evolutionary plane that leads directly to becoming divine. "You have always been because what it is that you are is God, or Divine Intelligence, but God takes on individual forms, droplets, reducing its power to small particles of individual consciousness…As that little form grows in power, in selfhood, in its own consciousness of self, it becomes larger and more Godlike. Then it becomes God." [30]

Because the realm of the soul is grounded in Light, and Conscious Light is equal to Divine Intelligence, every soul will eventually be 'enLightened,' says Zukav. Even a soul with no light, that is, operating only at the level of external power, will always come to know Light through the assistance provided to each soul. When one interacts out of the soul with the external world and with others, there is no judgment of right and wrong, only a searching for the feeling and source of the inappropriate behavior so as to transform it. Moral judgments belong to the realm of external power, the five senses (personality), and always result in competitiveness and violence. The source of all evil and violence is thus traced back to the soul where karma debts through previous negative use of power causes repetitive behavior. Healing and movement toward health cannot be achieved by moral imperatives nor even by psychological adjustment. Change and growth can only come about through the spiritual work of the soul which confronts its own bad karma and consciously chooses to change, that is, to willingly give up external power and activate the inner, authentic power of compassion, forgiveness and love.

How does one know how to make these choices and responses in the face of conflicts between the personality and the soul, as well as uncertainty as to what will actually result from a choice?

We are not alone, Zukav tells us. "Each human soul has both guides and Teachers. A guide is not a Teacher... Teachers operate on a more personal plane of involvement, so to speak, although they are impersonal energies that we personalize, that we feel a personal relationship with... The person who chooses to advance his or her spiritual growth, to cultivate awareness of his or her higher self, is on a vertical path."[31]

While the terminology is reminiscent of a more traditional concept of spiritual guidance, through divine revelation (Scripture=guide) and the Holy Spirit (Teacher), Zukav clearly does not want us to think of Teachers in the spirit world as having personality, or being personal. The Teacher serves as an impersonal prompter, providing energy to the soul which gives empowerment for the choice to move to a higher level of consciousness. Does one pray for guidance? Yes, answers Zukav. "Prayer is moving into a personal relationship with Divine Intelligence.... When you pray, you draw to you and invoke grace. Grace is uncontaminated conscious Light. It is Divinity." [32]

For many, Zukav's new age spirituality based on his concept of the soul offers a compelling alternative to the more traditional theological categories. This is especially the case for those who yearn for a personal religion freed from moral judgments, projection of guilt, claims for exclusivity, and authoritarian structures. The more traditional concept of original sin as inherited from the sin of Adam and Eve, for example, is retained in the concept of "karma debt which the soul must deal with from birth. Traditional theology taught that each person inherits a debt of guilt (original sin) for which one needs atonement, and which becomes the source of actual sin in each person's life. The new age spirituality of Zukav takes the concept of an inherited negative factor back beyond an original parent passed on to each succeeding generation and accounts for it through a reincarnation of the soul which carries with it negative karma.

No soul is born pure and 'full of Light.' The biblical story of the temptation of Adam and Eve in the garden 'to eat the forbidden apple,' as Zukav puts it, is actually an inevitable part of the evolution from the undifferentiated animal soul to a truly human soul. The soul without temptation and without struggle against the negative forces which strive against its Light is not a truly human soul. Thus, the emergence of the soul is necessarily accompanied by the struggle with negative karma.

What is appealing to many persons with this view is the fact that the soul should never feel guilty of wrong doing, either on the part of others or of oneself. Instead of moral judgment which disempowers the soul, Light comes into the soul to empower it for a journey which transforms the negative karma into positive enlightenment. The traditional concepts of sin and guilt have thus been replaced by an inherited deficit to the soul which does not require forgiveness nor atonement, but simply grace.

Grace, in new age spirituality, is associated with the Divine Intelligence which is freely accessible to all who choose the inner power of the soul over the external power of self-assertion. Grace does not presuppose sin and guilt, but simply a desire for enlightenment and growth. As in traditional theology, it is freely given and eventually effective for all souls, though not in any one soul's physical lifetime.

What traditional theology calls sanctification as the inward effect of the Holy Spirit, in new age spirituality is the evolution of the soul empowered by grace to move closer and closer to the Divine Intelligence which will eventually become the pure content of soul. Because the source of inappropriate and even violent behavior is due to negative karma in the soul, spiritual growth results in mental as well as emotional healing. Psychotherapy, unaided by the inner power of the soul, can only result in adaptation of personality and behavior to conform to external standards of what is considered normal. Similar to traditional theology, new age spirituality has no confidence in the capacity of psychology to understand and to heal the deeper conflicts of the soul. In contrast to traditional theology, however, new age spirituality does not pronounce judgement against the soul for its negative karma.

The threat of an individual's sense of the inevitability of death, which Ernest Becker saw as the underlying basis for all mental illness and emotional disorder, is overcome in new age spirituality by defining the soul itself as a 'piece of immortality' on the way to ultimate healing. If fear of death exists in the soul, it is considered to be a negative karma debt carried over from a previous incarnation. This fear tends to disempower the soul and needs to be understood and acknowledged in order to surrender it to the process of inevitable immortality. Death can only have power as an external force. The inner power of the soul can transform this negative karma, but only through a process of acknowledging the fear, consciously grasping it as a negative force, and choosing to deliver it over to the reality of immortal Light. The soul has a Teacher which provides the wisdom and energy to make this move. Failure to do so is not considered a weakness, for the soul does not judge but only awaits the moment to make another choice.

In this way, the core issues of life, the source of evil, personal guilt due to sin, redemption from guilt and sin, fear of death, and the longing for immortality are all dealt with in new age spirituality. Zukav thus provides the theological and philosophical framework for a new age theology through his concept of the soul.

Critics of Zukav point out that his writing on the soul has the appearance of a 'channeled text,' with a typical sense of assumed authority presented in an extreme *ex cathedra* mode, with no supporting evidence or reasoned argument. As a result, Zukav does not so much enter into conversation and dialogue with his reader, but lectures much like presentations one would hear at a retreat or conference. To the extent that his approach comes out of a kind of 'new age physics,' Zukav has been charged with presenting a new 'subjective science' picking up where traditional science leaves off. However, this mystical and subjective approach does not really build on any kind of scientific or empirical basis but breaks off into its own sphere of reality. "What if mystical 'enlightenment' is really a delusion?" asks one critic. "If supposed insights gained from such an enlightenment were incorporated into scientific theories, science would run aground! The world of the occult is brimming over with the fruits of 'subjective science'."[33]

My own view is that Zukav's version of the soul as the 'purifier' of the personality is something like spiritual liposuction. The soul purges the self of negative emotions and shapes the inner landscape of the self around the virtues of acceptance, compassion and self-affirmation. The self as contoured by the soul is trimmed of excess emotional weight resulting in a transformation that has cosmetic results but no cosmic significance. The self remains caught in a finite, temporal and mortal condition that will in the end, have the final say.

Recent studies of new age spirituality seem to agree that its distinctive element is some version of 'Self-spirituality.' The Self is viewed as sacred and by making contact with the intrinsic spirituality of the Self one becomes open to a spiritual world by which spiritual truth and spiritual teachers can 'channel' wisdom to the soul.[34]

Is this ultimately more satisfying than traditional

theology? It is certainly more convenient as measured against the demands of a more traditional theology and organized religion based upon it. And it is more congruent with the culture of narcissism in which it flourishes. To be assured that there is no ultimate moral judgment for personal behavior considered inappropriate by external social norms is good news, if not gospel. To be encouraged to become the architect and author of one's own spiritual growth is inspiring and freeing.

There is, of course, the matter of what we call personal, subjective identity, that is, the specific sense in which my history, with all of its pains and pleasures appears to be strongly lodged in what Zukav calls personality, not the soul. If what I call 'me' is really only a convenient vehicle for the more impersonal development and merging of the soul with Divine Intelligence, or immortal Life system, can this too be finally surrendered to an impersonal, undifferentiated ocean of divine Light? Am I not also deprived of true individuality if even the soul that possesses my external life is really only borrowed from the assembly line of souls moving relentlessly toward perfection?

In this sense was there not finally some logic to the members of the Heaven's Gate cult in San Diego who intentionally destroyed their bodies, which they called 'vehicles,' in order to join a celestial procession moving toward future perfection? And finally, is there not a remnant here, for all of the claim to be new age, of an older form of gnosticism which emerged in the latter part of the first century of the common era as an alternative to a more biblically based view of the soul? The Gnostics also made a distinction between a lower and higher self. The Gnostics also had a vision of a higher intelligence accessible only to those who were enlightened. Indeed, Zukav's distinction between the soul and the personality appears to be a contemporary version of the older gnostic depiction of the physical world as negative and the spiritual, or higher self, as positive. "Love is of the soul. Fear is of the personality," Zukav asserts.[35] In this way, the emotion of fear is not related to any objective reality, such as fear of God who punishes transgressions. Rather, it is the very *belief* that there is a God who holds humans morally and spiritually accountable that is the problem, in this way of thinking.

Matthew Fox, a contemporary Christian theologian and popular author identified with the new age movement, advocates a form of 'creation spirituality.' He suggests that the persistent teaching of the 'fall/redemption' motif in traditional theology fails to satisfy the contemporary spiritual seeker. "A devastating psychological corollary of the fall/redemption tradition is that religion with original sin as its starting point and religion built exclusively around sin and redemption does not teach trust... What if, however, religion was not meant to be built on psychologies of fear but on their opposite—on psychologies of trust and ever-growing expansion of the human person?" [36] The gospel according to Shirley MacLaine puts it this way: "We are not victims of the world we see. We are victims of the way we see the world. In truth, there are no victims."[37]

Should we be satisfied with such a form of spirituality which offers freedom from moral judgment only to evacuate the historical life of the soul of moral worth? But traditional concepts of the soul have been tested against the criteria of modern science as well as postmodern thought, and often found wanting. To raise these questions about the soul as viewed in the context of new age spirituality would be irresponsible without looking just as critically at what traditional theology has to say about the soul. We should reserve judgment until that is done.

THREE

The Divine Imprint of Soul:
Bearing The Birthmarks of Humanity

The soul is a God-created, God-nurtured, unique, developable, immortal human spirit. (M. Scott Peck)[38]

New Age spirituality is grounded in the self, often in the form of a mystical philosophy of mind and sometimes in the psychological depths of the soul. In either case, the boundary between the divine and the human becomes blurred or disappears altogether. The Judeo-Christian tradition, while viewing the human soul as bearing a divine imprint, makes a clear distinction between that which is human and that which is divine. In contrasting the new age view with the more traditional view of humans as spiritual beings, we can note many similarities but also significant differences.

In many ways, both New Age and biblical spirituality are more alike than different when viewed from the perspective of what spirituality means when experienced and practiced. The new age version of the soul, as we have seen, is potentially, if not actually, immortal, divine, and capable of transcending its mortal state as an earthbound creature. The biblical tradition speaks of human life as originating with a divine inbreathing which resulted in a 'living soul' (Genesis 2:7). Human being, as distinguished from all other forms of life, is said to bear the very 'image and likeness of God' (Genesis 1:26-27). In the biblical tradition, the gift of soul implies at least the promise of immortality as a future reality. New Age spirituality offers freedom from the tyranny of physical needs, stress and even disease. Through meditation, relaxation, and communion with the divine essence, persons experience healing, harmony and hope. Is this not also what God's people are promised in the Scriptures?

For example, The wisdom literature of the Old Testament describes the state of the righteous as one of peace, prosperity, freedom from anxiety, and perfect security in the face of adversity. The 'righteous,' as contrasted with the 'wicked,' are like "trees planted by streams of water, which yield their fruit in its season, and their leaves do not wither. In all that they do, they prosper" (Psalm 1:3). Jesus promised joy, peace and freedom from the 'cares of this world' to those who 'abide in him' like the branches abide in the vine (John 15:1-11). The Apostle Paul calls those who have become followers of Jesus as the Messiah 'saints' (literally 'holy ones'), and the 'living temple of God' (1 Cor 1:2; 2 Cor. 6:16).

In many ways, because the focus of New Age spirituality is upon the inner transformation of the self with immediate and short term effects of a subjective, or even physical nature, it offers a compelling alternative to the more traditional Christian spiritual disciplines. One can receive the benefits of New Age spirituality with no membership fees, no investment in organizational duties and responsibilities, and no institutional maintenance assessments! For every dollar invested one receives at least a book to hold in one's hand and access to the practical wisdom of celebrated and acclaimed spiritual teachers. Organized religion, on the other hand, needs contributing members not merely devoted followers.

In what way then does a more traditional, biblical approach still offer a distinctive alternative and a fulfilling lifestyle for the spiritual seeker? It is only when one looks for spiritual wisdom rather than merely a form of spirituality that one can answer that question. A spiritual power which offers health, prosperity and inner peace may yield an immediate blessing but result in an ultimate barrenness. Therapists tell me that many who experience emotional distress and mental disturbance seek immediate relief from pain rather than be willing to pursue a deeper healing which might require more pain. Ernest Becker has reminded us that 'denial of our mortality' offers short term relief from anxiety but at the cost of authentic existence as persons who must ultimately face their own death. A form of spirituality which masks the reality of our human finitude and limitation by assuming the 'character armor' of immortality is an 'illusion that lies.' It is spiritual folly.[39]

The gift of soul, as the biblical tradition reminds us, is not only what distinguishes us from all that is nonhuman, it is what makes us truly human as distinguished from God. Spiritual wisdom is the wisdom of life lived out of the soul as bearing the imprint of the divine, without being divine. The concept of the soul has experienced a theological rebirth in the womb of New Age spirituality. Not only has the malaise of our contemporary society been diagnosed as loss of soul (Thomas Moore), but one New Age author locates the source of spiritual power for the healing of our addictions in the 'seat of the soul' (Gary Zukav).

Can we talk about this? As long as the word 'soul' served only as a synonym for 'person,' and as a code word to express deeper psychological feelings and the intangible quality of a movement or group, we in the theological world could continue to talk and debate among ourselves as to its reality and meaning. Outside the halls of academic reflection and discourse, the language of personal piety as well as the liturgical language of the church and pastoral care continued to speak of the soul without having it 'die the death of a thousand qualifications.' Many of us were taught this bedtime prayer as children:

> Now I lay me down to sleep,
> I pray the Lord my soul to keep;
> And if I die before I wake,
> I pray the Lord my soul to take.

At the service of committal at the graveside one can still hear the measured cadence and reassuring rhythm of King James English: "Forasmuch as it hath pleased Almighty God to take out of this world the soul of our deceased brother, we therefore commit his body to the ground; earth to earth, ashes to ashes, dust to dust. . . "

"Naive and simplistic," says the philosopher. "Tell us what you mean by the word 'soul'." "Quaint and questionable," responds the scientist. "Tell us where to look for a 'soul'."[40]

The gravesite is not the place to quibble over what exactly has departed the corpse when the soul leaves, and what precise moment it made its ascent to God, leaving behind only the disposable body. Should questions arise in the mind of the curious, they are quickly suppressed by the acknowledgement that we are dealing with a mystery which can only unravel what little composure we have should we pursue them further. Like Job of old, in the face of the mystery of death and the soul, we say, "I lay my hand on my mouth. . . I have uttered what I did not understand, things too wonderful for me, which I did not know" (Job 40:4; 42:3).

There is a time and season for everything, the ancient sage reminds us. There is a "time to keep silence, and a time to speak" (Eccl. 3:1, 7). This is not a time for silence. It is a time to speak. If we are to speak of soul then we need to speak out of our tradition as well as to respond to a contemporary spiritual quest. The questions are not new nor our concerns outdated.

The Divine Imprint of Soul

The ancient teacher of wisdom in Israel, who called himself Koheleth, was a keen observer of the human condition. As he pondered and probed, he discovered more questions than answers. In a tone that betrayed both relentless cynicism and restless hope, he asked: "Who knows whether the human spirit goes upward and the spirit of animals goes downward to the earth?" (Ecclesiastes 3:21)

Who knows indeed! In former times, we might account for such ignorance as due to lack of scientific knowledge and philosophical precision. But how then would we account for the fact that today, some form of the same question tantalizes our scientists and torments our philosophers? Whether we call it spirit or soul, the question remains: what is it that makes humans both precious and perverse? What gives rise to our deepest religious insights but can also plunge us into the depths of guilt and despair?

Has the concept of a human soul disappeared in the presence of molecular biologists, clinical psychologists, and computer driven brain scans? Is the disappearance of the soul a consequence of our world 'come of age' or is it we who are lost and our souls doing the searching? Perhaps one indication that humans have a soul is that they appear to be the only creatures on earth that are thinking about it!

In modern times, the soul has been banished as the 'ghost in a machine' by some contemporary philosophers, and reduced to electronic impulses on the monitors of those who scan the human brain. If the soul has returned, for some it is as an alien creature, not a familiar friend. My own involvement in a research and book project led by a philosopher and psychologist explored the concept of the soul critically and cautiously. The conclusion turned out to be ambiguous and the concept of the soul quite elusive.[41]

Where should we begin? The Judeo-Christian tradition has a rich tradition of language and thought concerning the soul. The Scriptures of both the Old and New Testament serve as the primary source for this tradition. Unfortunately, when we look for precision with regard to the words used to describe the nature and components of the human person we find ambiguity and uncertainty. That there is something unique and precious about humans is unambiguous in this tradition. The difficulty is in submitting this quality of life to analysis.

My task as a theologian is to speak to the deeper yearnings and struggles of human existence as much as to bring to those existential human concerns some insights from the Word of God. It is for these reasons that I continue to use the word 'soul,' though with carefully nuanced and qualified meaning. I speak of soul as that which denotes the inner core of the whole person, including the body. By 'soul' I mean the personal and spiritual dimension of the self. Thus, the phrase 'body and soul' is not intended to suggest that the soul is something which is merely 'in' the body, or separate from the body, but the whole person with both an interior and an exterior life in the world.[42]

When we look at the biblical terms translated into English it quickly becomes apparent that there is little to be gained by attempting to construct a single portrait of human nature based on tracing the English word 'soul,' back to its original Hebrew and Greek language. The most we can say is that it would be wrong to conclude that the biblical term leads to any kind of dualism between the physical and non-physical dimension of the person.[43]

Those whom St. Paul describes as 'fleshly' (*sarkikos*) are also 'soulish' (*psychikos*). He never uses the body and the soul as contrasts for spiritual and unspiritual, or for mortal and immortal. Instead, he uses these terms to designate qualities of life expressed through both the physical and non-physical life. 'Spirit' and 'spiritual' signify a divine quality of life, received as a gift from God

The Divine Imprint of Soul

and having a share in God's Spirit (1 Cor 2:13-3:3). 'Flesh' and 'carnal' do not signify merely a natural or physical quality of life but a corrupt, self centered and mortal kind of life. It is not human nature that is the enemy of the spirit, but distortion or corruption of that human nature that is the enemy.

As a result we can say that the biblical terms for 'soul' (*nephesh*; *psyche*) are primarily functional rather than denoting discrete substances or entities. As such, while there are some distinctive patterns of use, the words used by the Bible to denote aspects of human life are not analytical and precise in a philosophical or semantical sense.

Is there then something about humans that possesses immortality and is not subject to death and destruction? The ancient Greeks tended to believe that there was, and they called this the immortal soul which only resided in the physical body as a temporary form of its existence, returning to an eternal form upon the death of the person. Socrates, as Plato records his conversations, is not the least perturbed over the fact of his own approaching death. He scoffed at the suggestion of his friends that he pay a small bribe and thereby escape death. "You are mistaken," he told them, "if you think that a man who is worth anything ought to spend his time weighing up the prospects of life and death. . . true philosophers make dying their profession."[44] For Socrates, death marked the freedom of the immortal soul as the bearer of the personality to escape the prison of the body and return to its blessed eternal state.

Scott Peck, in his attempt to reinstate the concept of a soul in the vocabulary of those who deal with mental and physical aspects of human mortality, defines the soul as follows: "The soul is a God-created, God-nurtured, unique, developable, immortal human spirit."[45] His purpose is to offer a more positive approach to old age and dying as a transitional process from self identity during a temporal life to continuing self-identity after death. He expresses no concern for any kind of existence prior to one's present life, such as in a theory of re-incarnation. His primary interest, he writes, is in life after death. "Whether we had a previous existence before our conception and birth seems to me an issue of relatively little consequence. On the other hand, the question of whether there is life after death—an afterlife—strikes me as absolutely crucial. If there is no afterlife, much of what I have been saying is rot."[46] His concept of an immortal spirit, however, needs to be looked at more closely in terms of biblical evidence.

The biblical view is that both soul and body were mortal and subject to destruction. Human persons are personal, embodied, mortal creatures created by God. The human soul is not an immortal substance encased in a mortal body. The life of the person (soul) emerges simultaneously with the bodily form of human existence. Human life has no existence independent of a body. Jesus warned, "Do not fear those who kill the body but cannot kill the soul; rather fear him who can destroy both soul and body in hell" (Matthew 10:28). The concept of an immortal soul is thus without clear biblical support.

Humans were created as mortal beings with a spiritual life contingent upon relation to God's Spirit, and thus subject to mortality and non-existence, apart from the divine intention and determination of God as creator and sustainer of human life. There is no warrant in Scripture for asserting that human nature bears some immortal, indestructible soul which has a natural capacity to survive death.[47]

What makes us a special person and in what does our sense of personal being consist? If we say the soul, yes, but the soul is not something separate from our historical self and our inner personality. The soul does not bear personal identity in isolation from one's embodied existence. As a result, continuity of the self does not rest upon an immortal soul that exists independently of the

The Divine Imprint of Soul

body and which leaves the body at death through its own immortal nature.

In this sense, one could say that each person has an identity that is more or less dependent upon the subjective life of the self, as well as an identity which is projected upon the person from and by the Spirit of God. For the Israelite, even the prospect of death and descent into the earth does not extinguish self-identity for, "if I make my bed in Sheol, you are there" (Psalm 139: 8). Self-identity arises as the subjective life (soul) of the body, and is grounded in the existence of the whole person as a unity. Even in our mother's womb, the Psalmist says, we were given personal identity by God:

> For it was you who formed my inward parts; you knit me together in my mother's womb. I praise you, for I am fearfully and wonderfully made. Wonderful are your works; that I know very well. My frame was not hidden from you, when I was being made in secret, intricately woven in the depths of the earth. Your eyes beheld my unformed substance. In your book were written all the days that were formed for me, when none of them as yet existed (Psalms 139:13-16).

What distinguishes the human from all other creatures is a spiritual orientation to and personal relation with God as Creator. One way of pointing to this distinctive is to recall that the texts which speak of the 'image and likeness of God' (Gen. 1:26-27; 5:1; 9:6) refer only to humans and not to non-human creatures. While the references to this divine image and likeness are rare in the Bible, the theme runs throughout Scripture (cf. Psalm 8:5; Hebrews 2:5-9). Humans are of "more value" than earth creatures (Matt. 6:26; 10:31; 12:9-12; Luke 12:24), and are the object of God's special concern (Hebrews 2:14-18).[48]

Humans are not described in Scripture as having a different earthly origin than animals, but that their existence as *human* creatures is qualitatively marked off from non-human creatures by the endowment of the divine image and the divine inbreathing.[49]

The soul is our birthmark as well as birthright. The

soul is the divine imprint upon human creatureliness which distinguishes us as humans as contrasted with both God and non-human creatures, animals as well as angels. "What are human beings that you are mindful of them," asks the Psalmist? "You have made them a little lower than the divine beings [angels]" (Psalm 8:4,5).

What is remarkable in this biblical vision of the human soul is that in being imprinted with the divine image it does not become divine but uniquely human. While New Age spirituality tends to divinize the soul, the biblical emphasis is on the humanity of the soul. New Age spirituality portrays the soul as in a process of evolution from a sub-human soul to a supra-human, divine, soul. In contrast, the Judeo-Christian tradition stresses the uniqueness of the human soul as differentiated both from the non-human and the divine. Where New Age spirituality creates a differentiation between the soul and personality with no essential likeness, the biblical vision creates a differentiation between the human embodied soul and God with the imprint of a likeness.

In the Judeo-Christian tradition the image and likeness of God can be understood as a capacity for relationship with the self, others and God in a knowing way, and an openness to a future which provides hope and meaning to life. The physical body itself is not held to be in the image of God, such that God has some aspect corresponding to the physical body of humans. Human beings as 'embodied souls' and 'besouled bodies' are in the image of God as upheld by the Spirit of God which attends and summons forth the human spirit.

In New Age spirituality the concept of the soul is not only sexless but also solitary. Sexual drives, distinctives and experiences are lodged in the external order of personality and physicality. The soul has compassion, but not passion of a sensual nature. The soul is autonomous and essentially anonymous in its purest form. In New Age spirituality the soul is an incarnation of undifferentiated soul even though it bears traces of its previous incarnation which it must transform and overcome. The soul touches other souls through compassion, openness and trust, but without a complementarity of being. There is no concrete and abiding social essence to the soul in New Age thought.

In the biblical account of creation the divine image is not possessed by the single individual; "it is not good that the man should be alone" (Gen. 2:18). Only when the man and the woman exist as complementary forms of human being is there a sense of completeness, "This at last is bone of my bones and flesh of my flesh;" (Gen. 2:23). The birthmark of a human soul is not its potential divinity, but its essential sociality. The spirituality of a human soul is not in its retreat from sensuality and sociality, but in its mutual reflection of divine love in human love and in mutual participation in the Creator's life through a creaturely human life.[50]

Elizabeth Barrett Browning was true to the Hebrew vision of the soul when she wrote:

> When our two souls stand up erect and strong,
> Face to face, silent, drawing nigh and nigher,
> Until the lengthening wings break into fire
> A either curvèd point,—what bitter wrong
> Can the earth do to us, that we should not long
> Be here contented. Think! In mounting higher,
> The angels would press on us and aspire
> To drop some golden orb of perfect song
> Into our deep, dear silence. Let us stay
> Rather on earth, Belovèd,—where the unfit
> Contrarious moods of men recoil away
> And isolate pure spirits, and permit
> A place to stand and love in for a day,
> With darkness and the death-hour rounding it.[51]

The creaturely human soul is never satisfied nor complete in a solitary vision of the divine. It is 'not good' to be a solitary soul, the Scripture tells us; 'at last,' there is another human soul to complete the divine image (Genesis 2:18, 23). The gift of soul may be what we have been searching for; it may be closer than we ever thought!

FOUR

The Community of Soul:
No One is an Island

I need you to be myself. This need is for a fully positive personal relation in which, because we trust one another, we can think and feel and act together. Only in such a relation can we really be ourselves. (John Macmurray)[52]

    The small rural community in the midwest where my parents were born, lived and died, had its own soul from which the several souls who made up the community received their nurture, daily sustenance, and meaningful destiny. Beyond that, I have stood at the grave site of my great grandparents in the mountain village of Bø in Norway, behind the 800 year old church in which my grandmother Kari was baptized and confirmed, before immigrating to the United States at the age of 16. She was the one from whom my father learned Norwegian as his first language—his mother tongue, as it were.

    I pondered the mystery of this woman, bearing centuries of life lived within the strict confines of faith and family within her own soul across an ocean, never to return. Never again to stand where I was now standing, never again to touch the face of father and mother, in life or in death. Was her soul secured through that amazing adventure by the tightly knit bond of relatives and friends who spoke the same language and ate the same food in the strange new land? No doubt. But within a single generation she made the transition to a new language, new food, and new grave sites to tend and became a soul of a new community.

My belief is that her soul was created with her own birth, unique and unused by any previous human or heavenly being. She was neither a reincarnation of a previous soul nor the incarnation of undifferentiated eternal soul. At the same time, I cannot rule out the effect of the souls of those who formed her ancestral community nor the souls of those who formed the community in which I discovered my own soul.

I believe that each human soul bears the birthmarks and imprint of the divine image and likeness. That is what makes it a human soul as distinguished from the souls of other creatures. Are there also birthmarks in our soul which bear the imprint of the soul of the community that bears and nourishes our life? It seems so. Not only do physical characteristics and even behavior patterns often bear resemblance to our biological parents, there also seem to be characteristics of the soul which are imprinted as birthmarks.

We often hear stories of identical twins who were separated at birth only to discover that when they are reunited as adults they have made almost identical choices in life. More than patterns of behavior and temperament which could be accounted for by personality factors, many of the astounding similarities have to do with virtual simultaneous decisions regarding dates of marriage, number of children, and types of automobiles purchased. Even if one attempts to account for this genetically, there remains a mystery which does not easily yield to empirical analysis. The uniqueness of each soul does not apparently demand the absence of some mutual imprinting, either by one as close as an identical twin, or what may even be just as close, the soul of the community which nourishes and sustains us.

I reflect upon my own parents, who discovered and fulfilled their own destiny, not as autonomous individuals or even as marriage partners, but as constituent parts of the community in which they lived. The community itself appeared to have what some have called, 'objective spirit,' and what I have called the soul of community. The intentional relation of two or more persons results in a structure of relation which becomes objective to the persons who created it. This is a sociological reality which can easily be experienced and demonstrated.[53]

Virtually any tightly knit community, such as the one in which I grew up, presents an enigma and even a barrier to one who enters as an outsider. The single school in that village was supplied by teachers who were hired from larger, more urban areas and, though they lived within the community, often for several years, they were never fully accepted. They were always viewed as 'teachers,' until such time as they set down their own roots in the community, or moved on. This is both the virtue and vice of such communities! The same cohesion that functions as the soul of the community can also lead to intolerance and even hostility toward others.

We lived for two years in Scotland, near a rural village with a small post office and local parish church. We attended the parish church regularly, and I preached there on several occasions. The woman who ran the small post office was well known to us as I saw her often and she also attended the church. We were well aware that our accent and 'Yankee' ways set us apart from the local community, though we made every attempt to fit in. As it came time for us to leave, the woman at the post office said, "We will miss you, as we were just getting accustomed to your face." We wondered how long it would be until our souls become as familiar as our face!

The bottom line, however, is that no soul can well develop in isolation from other souls, and the joys and sorrows of other souls have a grip on my own. This is what makes the lines written by the seventeenth century English poet, John Donne, so powerful and poignant: "No man is an Island, entire of its self; . . . any man's death diminishes me, Because I am involved in Mankinde; And therefore never send to know for whom the bell tolls; It tolls for thee."[54] Rabbi Lawrence Kushner, using a different metaphor, tells us much the same.

> Each lifetime is the pieces of a jigsaw puzzle.
> For some there are more pieces.
> For others the puzzle is more difficult to assemble.
> Some seem to be born with a nearly completed puzzle.
>
> But know this: No one has within themselves all the pieces to their puzzle.
> Everyone carries with them at least one and probably
> Many pieces to someone else's puzzle.
>
> And when you present your piece
> To another, whether you know it or not,
> Whether they know it or not,
> You are a messenger from the Most High.[55]

The soul of a community contours the moral boundaries and creates the core values of everyday life for its members. Gary Zukav in his New age version of the soul, speaks of the karma of a soul as a kind of relentless pattern of action and reaction. I prefer to speak of the soul of a community which both upholds the individual soul and makes demands upon it. The death of any member of the community made a demand that cut across all ethnic and religious differences. Participation in the rituals of death and dying was expected of every member of the community, even as all were prepared to contrib-

The Community of Soul

ute to the needs of one. Alvin Dueck suggests that the soul includes, "... notions of culture, community, and character..." that is "... capable of ethical discernment and religious character." Writing as a psychologist and therapist, he says "Therapists need a vocabulary and grammar of the soul that incorporates individual and communal dimensions."[56]

In his admonition to the church at Ephesus, St. Paul wrote: "Thieves must give up stealing; rather let them labor and work honestly with their own hands, so as to have something to share with the needy" (Ephesians 4:28). It is not enough for the soul of the thief to be 'saved' so that he is no longer stealing from others. He must contribute to the soul of the community by working so as to produce more than enough for himself and contribute to the needs of others. The so-called work ethic is not grounded in an impersonal sense of duty, nor ought one work for the sake of private virtue, but the soul of the community as represented in the common welfare of its members shapes the moral character of the soul.

How could one live one's life within such small confinement and have a sense of meaning and purpose? What satisfied the soul of those pioneers who struggled against the capricious elements of weather and suffered as many losses as gains in the gamble of seed against soil? My parents never spoke of this. I doubt that they ever thought much about it. If you have to search for something to satisfy the soul other than that for which you soul lives, there will be no ultimate satisfaction.

The value and worth of a soul is not an intangible quality to be debated by philosophers as though it were an abstract thing, apart from the soul itself. The soul has no existence in this lifetime other than the dust of the earth that bears it and ultimately reclaims it. But this dust has received the divine breath of life: "then the Lord God formed man from the dust of the ground, and breathed into his nostrils the breath of life; and the man became a living being" Genesis 2:7). As bearer of this 'breath of life,' the human soul has the imprint of a divine image and likeness. The Jewish scholar, Rabbi R. D. Hirsch suggests that the soul (*nephesh*) also bears the 'breath of life' (*neshama*). This 'breath of life' is unique to the soul of humans and, while borne by the 'dust soul' is not bound to the dust in the same way that the body is.[57]

The soul of community occurs on the plane of history and as a narrative of life and death carried forward by tradition, ritual and remembrance. This is the soul which bore the burden of the small souls of my parents, as well as all in that community. No individual soul should be expected to bear the burden of the meaning and value of life alone. A life lived out under the elongated shadow of others who have gone before, and a life which lays a foundation in that community for those who will follow will be satisfied and fulfilled.

When I approached the local bank with a request for a loan with which to begin my own farm operations in the community, I hardly knew how to present my case, as I had virtually no equity or collateral to pledge as a guarantee for the loan. When the loan officer at the bank heard my name, he immediately granted the loan solely on the good name of my father, who was hardly a wealthy man, having lost the only farm he ever purchased during the depression of the 1930s. "If you are Albert Anderson's son," he said, "your word is sufficient." In retrospect I realized that my deficit in material collateral was made up for by the 'soul collateral' which was not only earned by my father, but also which was banked in the community soul.

Where is the community bank of the soul for my own children? To paraphrase an African saying: "It takes a village to form a community bank for the soul." But the village no longer exists—at least for most of us. And, as the novelist Thomas Wolfe wrote, "We can't go home again." Our deficit is surely not in material things, even those that are not yet paid for. Our deficit is our loss of community for the soul.

"Two are better than one," wrote the ancient Sage of Israel, "because they have a good reward for their toil. For if they fall, one will lift up the other; but woe to one who is alone and falls and does not have another to help" (Eccl. 4:9-10).

The divine verdict upon the solitary human as described in the second Chapter of Genesis speaks of the deficit to an individual soul when there is not another for communion and community. "It is not good that the man should be alone; I will make him a helper as his partner" (Genesis 2:18). Biblical scholars proficient in the Hebrew language remind us that the Hebrew word for 'male' is not used in this account until there is a female. The word translated as 'man' in the English text is actually the word for 'earth creature.' Only when the woman emerges simultaneous with the man from the 'deep sleep' are the words for 'male' and 'female' used. There is thus no precedence of the male over the female, as both emerge in mutual encounter not only as humans but also in the complementary relationship of male and female.[58]

Not only is no soul complete in and of itself, it also is not simply a matter of adding another soul, so that 1 + 1 = 2. What was missing was not only another soul, but also the counterpart (partner) which one soul provides for the other. The equation is rather the reverse: 2=1; "Therefore a man leaves his father and his mother and clings to his wife, and they become one flesh" (Genesis 2:24). The simplicity and naiveté of the biblical story contains a profound and essential truth. The divine image as an imprint upon the human soul results in both a differentiation of one from the other and a complementary of being. The two are not formed with perfect symmetry—like two peas in a pod—but in perfect complementarity—like the meshing two gears which fulfill a common purpose.

We should not attempt to make too much out of the fact that the sexual differentiation of the two emerges simultaneously with their personal differentiation. At the same time, this does suggest that sexual differentiation and partnership has something to do with the soul and not only with biological equipment and function. The complementary structure of the human soul is itself an imprint of the divine being, who is neither male nor female, yet exists in a reciprocity of love. The human soul, however, has no existence except in biological life, with sexual differentiation written into every cell, including the brain.[59]

The concept of the soul in New Age spirituality as presented by Gary Zukav views the external order of physical and psychological life as only an expression of the soul, and not essential to the soul. Not only does this tend to individualize the soul, it treats the soul as asexual. More seriously, it views human sexuality as without a soul except that souls overcome the power of sex with the higher power of Divine Intelligence. This means that sexual disorders, not to mention sexual crimes, are the result of negative karma in the soul, which is not to be judged or viewed as a moral fault but only as a lower stage of soul development.

New Age spirituality has no vision of redemption for the soul because it attributes no moral or spiritual wrong to the soul. Is this what entices millions to abandon the traditional concepts of sin and salvation for the promised land of a spiritual utopia where New Age self therapy banishes guilt but still seeks grace? If so, then it ought to be remembered that the word 'utopia' originally mean 'no place,' not a beautiful place.

FIVE

The Redemption of the Soul: Whatever Became of Sin?

Happy are those whose transgression is forgiven, whose sin is covered. Happy are those to whom the Lord imputes no iniquity, and in whose spirit there is no deceit.
(King David)[60]

The soul explains, the personality blames. This is the gospel according to Gary Zukav, author of *The Seat of the Soul*, and the inner dynamic of new age spirituality. The personality threatens with guilt, the soul thrives on grace.[61] The personality needs atonement, the soul provides it by pushing through the negative karma in relentless pursuit of the underlying feelings which cause inappropriate behavior. This is the work which the soul must do and which only the soul can do. When the external order of society and the inward conscience assigns blame and demands, "You need to be punished," the soul patiently asks, "Why do I feel compelled to do these things?"

For New Age spirituality, when the soul seeks the cause of the feelings which explain behavior, it assumes personal responsibility but without moral judgment. The soul must take responsibility without assuming guilt, for guilt is disempowering and robs the soul of its grace. Whether one is accused of a moral fault by the inward conscience or by others, this is the horizontal, external power, lodged in the five senses. The soul has a multi-sensory capacity which operates on a completely different and higher level. "The person who chooses to advance his or her spiritual growth, to cultivate awareness of his or her higher self, is on a vertical path."[62] Those who think out of the external moral order find it difficult to explain immoral behavior without also finding moral fault and making moral judgments. For those who think this way, to explain immoral behavior without assigning guilt is the same as excusing it.

In an interview in the initial issue of the journal, *Today* (August, 1999), the wife of the President of the United States, sought to explain her husband's marital infidelity and promiscuous sexual behavior as caused by a dysfunctional family life which included emotional abuse by his mother and grandmother. Arguments raged in the media as to whether or not she was attempting to excuse his behavior and thereby absolve him of moral responsibility. In responding to questions about what she had said, she reiterated the fact that she was in no way excusing him, but rather explaining what had caused his problem and why he suffered such an impediment to personal and sexual responsibility. "He has a lot of work to do in that area," she said, "and he has not gone deep enough and worked hard enough on it."

In New Age spirituality, this 'soul work' requires grace, which is mediated directly to the soul as divine energy.[63] In this way of thinking we actually hinder the work of the soul and impede divine grace when we impose moral judgments on the soul due to inappropriate behavior caused by the negative karma. Compassion, understanding and encouragement can be given to persons in order to empower them to do the necessary work of transforming this negative karma. The one who continues to repeat inappropriate behavior has not 'gone deep enough and worked hard enough.' If one also says that one has forgiven another, as Mrs. Clinton said she had done with regard to her husband, in the terms of New Age spirituality this does not imply a moral fault but only a weak soul.

Whatever happened to sin?

This is a good question, and one asked many years ago by the well known psychiatrist, Karl Menninger, who authored a book by the same name.[64] Menninger is not alone among mental health professionals who lament the shift from personal guilt which requires confession, repentance and forgiveness, to attempts to explain immoral and inappropriate behavior as caused by deeper psychological and social factors outside of the person's control.

Given the choice between sin or sickness as the cause of human disorder, says O. Hobart Mowrer, former president of the American Psychological Association, sin may be 'the lesser of two evils.' Sin offers a more hopeful explanation because it opens up the way for 'radical redemption.'[65] Those who feel guilty and suffer from its effects, may actually be guilty, says Mowrer. Not all guilt feelings can be accounted for by the violation of an objective moral law, but when one feels that one is guilty of such a violation, atonement is necessary in order to remove the guilt.

In some cases, Mowrer reported, persons with sustained acute depression, after a period of time, let go of the depression saying that they felt that they had suffered enough and that this ought to make up for what they had done wrong. Depression, he concluded, may sometimes be a way of making atonement and until this is accomplished the patient will resist all attempts to remove guilt through psychotherapy alone. His conclusion was that redemption from sin as offered in the traditional Judeo-Christian tradition had therapeutic merits as well as spiritual meaning.

Does the human soul need redemption? And if so, how is it to be achieved?

The concept of atonement in the biblical literature is not only related to the fact of sin as something that places human beings under divine judgment, it has something to do with the soul. Not only does the Scripture speak of sin when it speaks of the soul, but it also speaks of sacrifice and of blood.

"For the life of the flesh is in the blood; and I have given it to you for making atonement for your lives [souls] on the altar; for, as life [soul], it is the blood that makes atonement" (Leviticus 17:11). The Hebrew word for soul (*nephesh*) in this text is translated by most modern versions of the Bible as 'life,' rather than 'soul.' It denotes persons in their entirety, not merely the 'soul' that is subject to the penalty of death due to sin. As in many other biblical texts, the word soul is used as a synonym for human life viewed from the perspective of accountability before God.

Up to the time of Jesus, as long as there was a temple in Jerusalem where animal sacrifice could be offered, blood was shed as a vicarious redemption of the souls (lives) of the Hebrew people under the divine covenant as instituted by Moses. This covenant came to be known as the 'covenant of blood' for "without the shedding of blood there is no remission of sins" (Hebrews 9:20, 22). The first century Christian community, composed at first of Jews who accepted Jesus as the promised Messiah, also came to understand that his death and the shedding of his blood on the cross completed, once and for all, this sacrificial ritual. Through the death of Jesus on the cross, a 'new and better covenant' was instituted through the shedding of his own blood, 'thus obtaining eternal redemption' (Hebrews 9:12).

The effect of this was to put an end to the shedding of blood as a means by which human souls could be redeemed from the effects and penalty of sin. Thus we "have

The Redemption of the Soul

confidence to enter the sanctuary by the blood of Jesus" and can approach God in "full assurance of faith, with our hearts sprinkled clean from an evil conscience..."(Hebrews 10:19,22).

Traditional Christian theology developed its doctrine of the atonement on the necessity of sin being forgiven by God, and the new covenant through Jesus Christ as the perfect and completed offering to God of all that the old covenant through Moses had provided. Two aspects of the atoning significance of Jesus Christ became distinctive for later theologians attempting to explain how this was accomplished.

First, there was an emphasis on the shedding of blood as a requirement for the removal of sin as objective guilt. The removal of objective guilt through the blood of Christ then had its subjective effect in cleansing, or freeing the human soul from the guilt and the power of sin.

Second, with a rather different view of sin as 'dishonor' to God, Anselm of Canterbury (1033-1109), viewed the sacrifice of Christ and the shedding of his blood on the cross as making full 'satisfaction' to God's honor and thus freeing God to pardon sin without violating his own sense of justice. While the blood of Christ was still viewed as the necessary and efficacious component of this theory, the effect was not such upon human souls but upon God. Orthodox Christian theology adopted this view for the most part, making the cross on which Jesus died the point at which the atonement was completed as an objective basis for God's offer of grace freely, to be received through repentance and faith. The actual subjective effect on human souls was then attributed to the mediation of saving grace, through sacraments or, as many churches following the 16th century Reformation, directly and freely through faith alone.

In this view, there was no question but that human souls were in need of redemption from sin, both that of the original parents, Adam and Eve, as well as their own. There was no question but that the shedding of the blood of Christ on the cross effected an objective basis for atonement and rendered full satisfaction to God's moral justice and honor.

Nonetheless, questions were raised.

Horrified at the teaching that God needed the shedding of blood by a human sacrifice in order to be appeased, Abelard (1079-1142) protested: " . . . how cruel and wicked it seems that anyone should demand the blood of an innocent person as the price for anything, or that it should in any way please him that an innocent man should be slain—still less that God should consider the death of his Son so agreeable that by it he should be reconciled to the world."[66]

Five centuries later, Socinus, could be equally blunt: "Why should God have willed to kill his innocent Son by a cruel and execrable death, when there was no need of satisfaction? In this way both the generosity of the Son perishes, and, instead of a most benign and munificent God, with supreme impiety and unspeakable sacrilege, we concoct for ourselves a God who is base and sordid."[67]

Many contemporary Christians, without having read either Abelard or Socinus, have abandoned the concept of a blood sacrifice as worthy of a loving and gracious God. While viewing the human soul as in need of grace due to personal sin, they view the soul as inherently good and capable of making moral and spiritual growth with the aid of divine grace. If there are indeed millions of people today who are attracted to some form of NewAge spirituality, those who have abandoned the more traditional view of sin and atonement through the sacrificial life and death of Christ may well be found among them.[68]

In new age spirituality the soul itself is in the process of redemption thorough its several stages or cycles of incarnation. As the soul grows in Light, it overcomes the negative karma in the personality, which might be called 'sin.' One could say that the soul has become the redeemer of the human race through its incarnation in millions, if not billions, of individuals. This is a redemption without blood, without guilt, and without appeasing a wrathful deity. Jesus is one of the 'purest souls' to have existed and thus can serve as an exemplar, if not an actual redeemer.

If we can set aside the Bible as itself being a product of primitive and 'unenLightened souls,' then why should we not be satisfied with the spirituality of the New Age movement? Is the problem, and I must confess there is one, merely our view of the Bible or our view of the soul? I suggest that it is both, but that the issue of what constitutes the soul is the key to how we read and view the Bible.

Look once again at the text with which we began this discussion. "For the life of the flesh is in the blood; and I have given it to you for making atonement for your lives [souls] on the altar; for, as life [soul], it is the blood that makes atonement" (Leviticus 17:11). To say that the life of the flesh is in the blood is not to say that blood itself has a mystical or spiritual quality, but that when the blood flows out of the body one's life is extinguished. In a primitive society without the aid of modern science, one cannot live without blood, and when the blood escapes the body, death results. It is as simple as that. It would be absurd to think that a bowl of animal blood sprinkled upon the ancient altar without the death of the animal would constitute any kind of sacrifice. Nor would the blood of Jesus, if it could somehow have been withdrawn had any power to cancel out sin apart from the death of Jesus himself.

The word 'soul' (*nephesh*) is a synonym for life and represents the whole person—"my soul thirsts for God (Psalm 42:2)—not merely nonphysical entity. The result of human sin according to the biblical account is not merely that one becomes a 'sinner' or an immoral person, but that one actually suffers 'death' with respect to a 'life before and with God' (Genesis 2:17).

The great human dilemma is not merely sin, but death. Neither the death of an animal nor the death of a person can itself overcome death; it can only bring life to a conclusion as a final fatal event. It is life that overcomes death. Only life given to the soul can restore it from the sentence of death which is the inevitable end of the soul apart from new life given to it by God. The effect of the atonement for the Hebrews under the old covenant was not merely the removal of sin as an objective guilt, but more importantly the granting of life to their own souls on the basis of another life taken.

This is why the contemporaries of Jesus were revived in their own spirits by his resurrection from the dead and their encounter of him as a living soul with a resurrected body. The apostle Paul put it plainly, "If Christ has not been raised, your faith is futile and you are still in your sins" (1 Corinthians 15:17). The redemption of the soul of Jesus was not attained through his 'higher self' nor by divine Light which flooded his soul. Rather, the redemption of his soul was through the resurrection of his soul by God out of death, that is, his entire person from the grave.

A Christian view of the soul is determined by how we read the Bible. It must be acknowledged that many NewAge writers also cite the Scriptures, but read it quite differently. One is reminded of the words of William Blake:

> The vision of Christ that thou dost see
> Is my vision's greatest enemy.
> Thine has a great hook nose like thine;
> Mine has a snub nose like to mine.
> . . . .
> Both read the Bible day and night,
> But thou read'st black where I read white.[69]

The Redemption of the Soul

The Hebrew people understood their Scriptures (what we call the Old Testament) as emerging from their encounter with God as one who called them forth from all of the families of the earth and constituted them as a community of witness to the revelation of God's being and human nature and destiny. Their view of God emerged from their encounter with God as the redeemer of their souls. The redemption of the soul therefore precedes the creation of the soul in their understanding of themselves and God. The one who redeemed their souls out of bondage and oppression in Egypt through the exodus event was definitive for their understanding of this same God as their Creator.

Humans emerged from the dust of the ground by receiving the 'gift of soul' (Genesis 2:7). This marks the beginning of the human soul as embodied, personal and communal life. The redeemed soul is already granted life out of death. In a similar way, the origin of the soul is the gift of life out of the dust. This is why the Hebrews did not ascribe immortality to the soul as did the Greek philosophers. Immortality is not the soul's property, but it is the soul's privilege through divine promise.

Human destiny beyond returning to the dust of the ground is likewise not a philosophical problem for the Hebrews. The God who is the redeemer of souls will not abandon the soul to Sheol (the underground): "For you do not give me up to Sheol, or let your faithful one see the Pit" (Psalms 16:10). "O Lord, you brought up my soul from Sheol, restored me to life from among those gone down to the Pit" (Psalms 30:3). Beyond that, the Hebrews had no clear vision of personal existence beyond death, though they could yearn for it.

With this understanding of soul, we can read the Bible when it speaks of sin and its consequences within the context of the redemption of the soul as its established state by divine grace and power. The soul is not at its core sinful, but graceful. Fallen into spiritual disarray, the biblical view of humanity is one of spiritual disgrace, moral disobedience, and psychological ambivalence. The apostle Paul can affirm that deep within his inmost self there is a love for God, and yet confess that he is caught in hopeless moral ambivalence and spiritual disorder (Romans 7). Nonetheless, he speaks of his soul as already 'without condemnation' and alive by the indwelling Spirit of God (Romans 8).

It is the Spirit of God which makes the soul alive. It is life lived through the indwelling Spirit of Jesus Christ which constitutes the spirituality of the soul. This is atonement and redemption which looks back at the cross and the death of Jesus Christ, not to see the blood, nor to see the shadows pass from the face of an angry God, but in gratitude for the life which comes out of death.

This is a quite different soul than the one described by Gary Zukav, and a different version of spirituality from that offered by the philosophy of the New Age. Is it, however, more satisfying and more truthful? We shall see.

SIX

The Spiritual Nature of the Soul:

Living with Faith, Hope and Love

We are not human beings having a spiritual experience, but spiritual beings having a human experience.
(Pierre Teilhard de Chardin)[70]

There is something about the human spirit that defies explanation. We all know people whose spirit refuses to give up, who are moved by some invisible force that gives them a vision of a future which gives meaning and purpose for the present.

Allen is such a person. Suffering a spinal cord injury in a motorcycle accident that left him paraplegic, he saw his dream of becoming a professional athlete crash and burn. When suicidal thoughts crept in during the early weeks of his hospitalization, he battled them with a will to live that had no content or purpose. Without a means of making a living, he chose life. Without the means of caring for himself, he accepted care from others as a way of life. Drifting in the twilight zone of an ambiance that excused him from having to lift as much as a finger (literally!), he felt the air begin to move his wings (figuratively) and his spirit began to rise.

Having a nodding acquaintance with God through an untested and untroubled childhood faith, he began to respond to the trauma of his paralysis, and directed some pointed questions to the invisible deity that lurked around the edges of his consciousness. "All right God," he said one day, "You created the world out of nothing, let's see what you can do with me!"

In recounting this, Allen said that for the first time in his life, he viewed God as someone he could talk to without having to be sure of using the right words. "After all," he said, "What more could God do to me? If he didn't like it he could just turn away and leave me alone. I was not in a position to cause him any trouble."

As it turned out, he didn't get any answer, no disembodied voice came to him with the cosmic vibes of a Charlton Heston. Nothing. But a strange stirring in his own spirit took place. "I felt like part of me had wings, " he said, "and I was lifted by an invisible breath so that I could see my situation from a different perspective. I gained a vision for what I might do within the limitations of my physical disability, and found a new hope for my life."

When he was released from the rehabilitation unit and able to use a wheelchair, he enrolled in a program leading to a doctorate in clinical psychology, and is now a licensed therapist.

Recently, I asked him a purely theoretical question. "Allen, if you had a chance to go back and live that tragic moment over again, and escape the accident, retaining your original physical ability, would you choose to do that?"

"That is really hard to answer," he responded slowly. "But to do so would annihilate the person that I have now become. I had thought my identity was going to be found through my profession; now it is my possession. I have become all that I could have hoped for—what more can one ask of life?"

That is Allen's story. His soul was moved, I believe, by the Spirit of God and he gained the spiritual power of hope. Early in his life he hoped to find fulfillment and satisfaction through the attainment of a boyhood dream. When he awoke, his life was a nightmare and that hope died. "I felt like part of me had wings," he said, "and I was lifted by an invisible breath so that I could see my situation from a different perspective." While his legs remain paralyzed, the wings of his spirit carry him farther than he ever dreamed possible.

From his story I discovered the meaning of the prophet's poetry: "Even youths will faint and be weary, and the young will fall exhausted; but those who wait for the Lord shall renew their strength, they shall mount up with wings like eagles, they shall run and not be weary, they shall walk and not faint" (Isaiah 40:30-31).

I learned that the spiritual nature of the soul is not an aspect of its divinity, but of its humanity. This is what differentiates the biblical concept of the soul from that of New Age spirituality. My attempt has been to redefine the soul as that which each person possesses as the gift of human life, endowed with the divine image and likeness. The soul is not a higher aspect of the self, nor a nonphysical 'substance' operating in a body or human personality. The soul is the person in totality, fully human but also determined by the Creator God to possess a spirituality that is only possible through communion and communication with God.

The soul of Allen was stirred to its depths by the tragic circumstances that reduced his body to virtual helplessness. Out of that experience he discovered a vision of what he could accomplish within the limitations of permanent paralysis. He describes it as 'being lifted by an invisible breath.'

The Hebrew word for spirit is 'breath' (*ruach*), as is the Greek word for spirit (*pneuma*). The Genesis account of creation uses the same word when it describes the formation of humanity out of the dust of the ground: "...then the Lord God formed man from the dust of the ground, and breathed into his nostrils the breath [*ruach*] of life; and the man became a living being [*nephesh*]" (Genesis 2:7). In this text, the word breath is used as well as the word for soul. The human soul as embodied existence has a core of spirituality which pervades the whole of life.

The spiritual life of the soul is not a higher form of the self gained by moving beyond the five senses into another realm of consciousness. When Allen spoke of the experience which turned him back into the real world with a new vision of what he could accomplish despite his severe limitations, he used the metaphor of 'wings' and of 'being lifted up' so as to gain a new perspective of his situation.

As it turned out, this was not primarily a religious experience for him though it was deeply spiritual. There was no miracle which produced healing at the physical level for which he could credit God. At the same time, he did experience a healing of the soul which resulted in the integration of 'body and soul' as demonstrated in the purpose and mission that empowered him to live and function with his disability. He experienced a spiritual healing of the soul which transformed a disability into an ability and allowed him to live normally in a society which is abnormally filled with hatred, pain, and loneliness. His newly discovered spirituality did also result in a new quality of faith and relationship with God which he considers more authentic and truthful than the simple 'truths' which he professed innocently and naively in earlier years.

New Age spirituality might account for his experience as typical of those who actualize the hidden spirituality of the self to produce spiritual healing in the face of adverse and limiting conditions. I could agree up to that point, for there is a human dimension to the soul's spirituality that may not have any specific religious in-tent or content. There is a place for emotional, mental and even physical wellbeing and health which has a deeply spiritual core. The human soul has an intrinsic spiritual nature that has a drive toward health and wholeness.

Psychologist Robert Grant has studied the effects of trauma on victims of work place accidents, violence, rape and war. In his research he found that a traumatic experience can break a person, destroying trust in God and the world. Or it can provide a spiritual opening—a crack that opens the way to a deeper sense of life's meaning. Human beings, he says, have a tremendous resiliency under such conditions and discover spiritual depths that lead to greater faith and hope than they have every known. Not all have this experience, he admits, but it is more common than we realize.

From his studies, Grant concludes that there are many people who experience what he calls 'trauma spirituality.' When the fundamental beliefs and concepts upon which people have built their lives crumble and fall apart, some people take a walk through the 'metaphysical minefields' brought on by traumatic experience and emerge with an altered consciousness and new access to their spiritual core.

The language and concepts expressed by Grant are very similar to concepts of spirituality expressed by writers and thinkers in the new age movement. While he does not use the word soul, his view of the self includes a spiritual core that sounds very much like the concept of the soul used by Gary Zukav, as I have discussed earlier. What Grant describes also fits very closely to what I have observed in my friend Allen, whose own trauma experience led to a new kind of spirituality amidst the ruins of his more traditional concepts of faith and God.

What these experiences have in common is a view of the self that has its own source and capacity for a life of the spirit which transcends the feelings of anger, bitterness, despair and emerges with a vision of life as having new meaning and purpose. I grant the validity of such experiences, but then ask, "Is the human soul the center of the self and the source of a spirituality which remains unscathed by outrageous evil and inexplicable fate?"

According to Gary Zukav, the answer is yes. He then proceeds to define the human soul as a 'droplet' from the ocean of immortal soul which has within it the energy and power of divine soul; that is, the soul only resides in the human but is not completely human. The soul, in fact, is a form of God: "God takes on individual forms, droplets, reducing its power to small particles of individual consciousness...As that little form grows in power, in selfhood, in its own consciousness of self, it becomes larger and more Godlike. Then it becomes God."[72]

Why should we not be content with that? Why should we not agree that a spirituality of the soul that results in the healing of a broken spirit and the recovery of purpose and meaning in life is a sufficient form of faith? And what hinders us from viewing this concept of God as more satisfying to the soul than one which locates a divine being outside of our existence and unavailable when we most are in need?

If my friend Allen, with his 'disability,' has found spiritual healing for his soul which gives him the inspiration and faith to find and fulfill a mission in life beyond that of the most 'able' persons, does he also need redemption for his soul and faith in a God who is also his savior? If it isn't broken, don't try and fix it, goes the old adage.

What concerns me, however, is not attempting to fix what isn't broken, but missing the whole by looking only at a part. A piece of a broken stained glass window can still serve as a prism through which can view the soul as a 'many splendoured thing.'

"The angels keep their ancient places;—
Turn but a stone and start a wing!
'Tis ye, 'tis your estranged faces,

The Spiritual Nature of the Soul

That miss the many-splendoured thing."[73]

As I see it, the problem arises when the soul becomes its own 'center' of spirituality and health. Without a center which lies outside of the self, said theologian Emil Brunner, there is a 'sorrow of heart' which experiences ultimately the disharmony of existence. To attempt to organize the self around its own center, warned Brunner, produces what might be called spiritual or psychological health, but without a center which gives the self a place of hope in God beyond oneself, this 'health' is itself a form of madness, or insanity. "To place the central point of existence outside God, who is the true Centre, in the 'I' and the world, is madness; for it cannot be a real centre; the world cannot provide any resting-place for the Self; it only makes it oscillate hither and thither."[74]

The human soul is mortal, not immortal, though it has the promise of immortality. The spirituality of the human soul originating in the soul itself is mortal, bound to this temporal life span. Even as such, it can be a spirituality of amazing courage in the face of danger and difficulty, of inspired patience in living with unresolved conflict and suffering, of unqualified optimism in believing that all things will work out for the best, and of creative imagination by overcoming brokenness and barrenness with vision and vitality. All of this, yes. But all the while, living with the 'sorrow of heart' which Brunner reminds us attends the soul as it faces its own mortal existence. The 'Denial of Death,' as Ernest Becker described it in his book by the same title, is a façade of spirituality draped over the skeleton of the soul entombed quietly behind the most audacious pretense of immortality.[75]

As we saw in the previous chapter on the redemption of the soul, the deepest human dilemma is not sin as a moral defect, but death as a spiritual demise. The human soul retains remnants of its spiritual core received as a divine 'breath of life.' This remnant can produce a form of spirituality which does not need the authentication of formal theological concepts to verify it. This becomes a compelling seduction into the power of New Age spirituality.

For New Age spirituality the soul is the source of the healing rather than the recipient of health. The soul, as Gary Zukav has written, is but the reduction of an 'immortal Life system' into the framework of a temporary human receptacle. Conceiving of the soul as immortal rather than mortal, and divine rather than human, is one answer to the dilemma of human mortality. New Age spirituality also speaks of faith, hope and love. But in this case the object of faith has dissolved into faith itself, the ground of hope has become the 'seat of the soul,' and the personal character of love has drowned in the impersonal ocean of the soul without a name and face.

The biblical account of the temptation which came to the first humans was framed in the form of a suggestion that spirituality was something to be claimed as a prerogative of the soul. "God knows that when you eat of it your eyes will be opened, and you will be like God . . . " (Gen. 3:5). When they ate the forbidden fruit, they gained a kind of spiritual autonomy and freedom from dependence upon God. Human spirituality can trace its origins back to this fatal step away from God and a flight into the soul of the self as a vestige of the divine image and likeness. New Age spirituality is as old as the attempt to 'be like God.' Perhaps this is why human spirituality, for all that it can achieve as evidenced by Allen's pilgrimage, is resistant to the suggestion that the soul is not immortal and apart from the gift of life, can only make an idol shaped in its own image.

The biblical vision of the soul and of human spirituality is quite distinct from that of the New Age version. Authentic spirituality of the human soul must have its

The Spiritual Nature of the Soul

origin in something other than itself. Faith must have an object in order to avoid fanaticism and foolishness. Hope must have a promise to escape the betrayal of the soul by the senses. Love must have a partner rather than merely being a passion.

The longing of the soul for immortality is not itself a mark of immortality, but rather of mortality. At the same time, this longing becomes the subjective reach of the soul for its objective counterpart. In his distress of soul due to unrelenting pain for which there was no explanation or justification, Job asks, "If mortals die, will they live again? All the days of my service I would wait until my release should come. You would call, and I would answer you; you would long for the work of your hands" (Job 14:14-15).

Job not only longed for release from his anguish but also the longed for some sign that his God longed for him. Later, he could even claim, "Even now, my witness is in heaven, and he that vouches for me is on high" (16:19). And finally, his hope has become faith, "For I know that my Redeemer lives, and that at the last he will stand upon the earth after my skin has been thus destroyed, then in my flesh I shall see God, who I shall see on my side, and my eyes shall behold and not another [or 'not a stranger']" (19:25-26). Job's family and friends had abandoned him, but he longed for and believed in a God who loved (longed for) him and who would appear finally, not as a stranger, but as a friend.

The spirituality of the soul comes to expression not only as hope which is objectively grounded in God, but also as a deeply felt value of the self. Hope is the vision which is seen with the eyes of faith and is the promise that satisfies the deepest longing of the soul.

While hope must have its center in God, as Brunner suggests, its value must be realized and felt in the soul. When we have discovered the longing which fuels faith and inspires hope, we have learned its value. For a faith which does not arise from this unquenchable hunger for life is not faith but fantasy. There is a cosmic disposal for beliefs which have lost their value and been discarded. Without the value of hope, faith can lose its own value and collapse back into despair. We are not born with the value of hope, but it can be learned.

Consider Jesus. In his conversation with the Samaritan woman at the well, he said, "If you knew the gift of God, and who it is that is saying to you, 'Give me a drink,' you would have asked him, and he would have given you living water." The woman protested, "Sir, you have no bucket, and the well is deep. Where do you get that living water?" Jesus responded, "Everyone who drinks of this water will be thirsty again, but those who drink of the water that I give them will never be thirsty. The water that I will give will become in them a spring of water gushing up to eternal life." He thus touched the core of this woman's passion, which hitherto, had been indiscriminately poured out in a series of unfulfilling relationships. What others may have seen as promiscuous sexual passion, Jesus diagnosed as an unfulfilled thirst for a love that gave back as much as it took. She cried out, "Sir, give me this water, so that I may never be thirsty or have to keep coming here to draw water." (John 4:1-15) Practical as she was, a thirst had been opened up in her which would soon become faith.

In his own life, Jesus revealed a consuming hunger for fulfillment which drove him ever deeper into his mission to go to Jerusalem and present himself as Israel's messiah. When it became clear that this was leading directly to danger, Jesus cried out: "I have come to bring fire to the earth and how I wish it were already kindled! I have a baptism with which to be baptized, and what stress I am under until it is completed" (Luke 12:49-50). This is a faith fueled by hope.

The author of the book of Hebrews recognized both the hunger and the hope which Jesus had when he summoned us to look to Jesus, "the pioneer and perfecter of our faith, who for the sake of the joy that was set before him endured the cross, disregarding its shame, and has taken his seat at the right hand of the throne of God" (Heb. 12:2). Jesus learned the value of hope as an anchor for his own soul when exposed to the assaults against him. Without the hunger for an ultimate joy he would have chosen a more accessible goal and settled for some form of immediate success. He had plenty of invitations and a score of opportunities to do just that. Without hope as the 'lodestar' of his faith, he would have fallen into the shame of despair and been consumed by the very faith that compelled him forward.

The author of Hebrews writes with pastoral concern, so that those who are awakened to the value of faith may have that faith grounded in a hope that will abide. "We have this hope, a sure and steadfast anchor of the soul, a hope that enters the inner shrine behind the curtain, where Jesus, a forerunner on our behalf, has entered, having become a high priest forever, . . . " (Heb. 6:19-20).

If faith has its value lodged in the self's hunger and longing for life's deepest joy, where do we locate hope? For hope to have value it must also be resident in the soul, not merely held in the mind as an abstract concept. If hope is to be a 'steadfast anchor of the soul,' as the author of Hebrews put it, it must be experienced in the self alongside of faith. For hope to have value it must be more than a statement of what one believes. It must be a resident hope, not an alien hope.

To be sure, the **content** of hope lies outside of the self, in God as Brunner has said, and more specifically in Jesus Christ, as the author of Hebrews has testified. It is the content of hope upon which faith finally rests. Without this content, assured by the very reality of God and made manifest through the life, death and resurrection of Jesus Christ, hope shatters like glass under the impact of the 'slings and arrows of outrageous fortune,' as

Shakespeare so eloquently put it. But this hope is alien to many people because it does not **abide** in the soul as the counterpart of faith.

As I write this, the morning newspaper tells a tragic story of an 81 year old man who shot his 78 year old wife in the patio of their home, and then turned the gun on himself as horrified neighbors watched. A friend of the couple reported that the man had recently shared his concern about the evidence of approaching Alzheimer's disease on his wife. "Who will take care of her if I die?" he worried. On the other hand, others told of their close relationship, their daily walks and journeys to the market as though nothing was wrong. In retrospect, it appears that with no hope for a future the man lacked the vitality of faith necessary to live a life which even in the present time gave them opportunities for enjoyment and shared love. This reveals the close relationship between hope and faith. Without some anchor of hope, faith faltered and led to the desperate act of murder and suicide as the only alternative.

When Jesus appeared to his disciples following his resurrection, we are told that he "breathed on them and said to them, 'Receive the Holy Spirit'" (John 20:22). He thus prepared them to have the assurance of their own shared destiny with him through the indwelling spirit of hope. Peter begins his first epistle by reminding us that God, through his great mercy, "has given us a new birth into a living hope through the resurrection of Jesus Christ from the dead, . . ." (1 Peter 1:3). Paul writes that "hope does not disappoint us, because God's love has been poured into our hearts through the Holy Spirit that has been given to us" (Ro. 5:5).

From this we can conclude that hope, which is anchored in Jesus Christ as the one who lives and by whom we can have assurance of eternal life, arises in the human self as the Spirit of God moves within us. There is a created human spirit which is given by God through the mystery and miracle of birth, but there is also the Spirit of God, or the Spirit of Christ, which is communicated to the self and experienced as the power of spirit within the self.

This is a vision of the soul and the spiritual life of the soul which is not satisfied with a retreat from mortal life into the 'higher self,' as some forms of New Age spirituality offer. The soul may have wings, to use one metaphor, but it also has a body which, even if it cannot walk, must carry forth the soul into life. Keith Miller extends spirituality to the entire spectrum of our earthly life: "Spirituality begins with the renewing and satisfying of the soul, and extends to every aspect of the Christian's life before God and others. . . . In reality, spirituality encompasses all that we are and do—our Christian beliefs, heart connection to the Lord, relationships with others, how we use our money, our concern for the environment, and so on."[76]

My friend Allen is sustained by a spirituality which provided healing for his soul and a meaningful purpose for his life though he continues to suffer paralysis of his body. Following the accident which resulted in his injury he found the traditional formulas of faith hollow and hopeless. When he could not find answers from God, like Job of old, he made demands. As a result he began a journey toward spiritual health which led to a new vision of hope and a new dimension of faith. Finding a partner in love (he is now married), he is beginning also to find a spiritual partner in God. While his spiritual journey is new, it is also as old as that of Job and creative as that of Jesus. He has accepted the mortality of his soul as the context for a life of meaning and purpose within the confining limits of a body which only moves as far and fast as his hands and wheels will take him.

There is a partnership between the human spirit and the Spirit of God which begins with the gift of the Spirit to the soul, which causes hope to arise and faith to emerge, resulting in the abiding experience of God's love. Exploring this partnership enlarges the soul and broadens the vision of life.

SEVEN

The Companion of the Soul:
Creative Partnering With God

The human heart can go to the lengths of God...
Affairs are now soul size. The enterprise
is exploration into God. (Christopher Fry)[77]

The legend of Cuthman, Saint of Sussex, became a charming and captivating story as told by the English playwright, Christopher Fry. In *The Boy With a Cart*, the shepherd boy Cuthman spends his days alone guarding his father's sheep. When he is tired, the boy charges God to watch his sheep while he sleeps. God never fails. When his neighbors come to tell him that his father has died, the boy cries out in anguish, "Did I steal God away from my father to guard my sheep? How can I keep pace with a pain that comes in my head so fast?"[78]

Returning to his home, he discovers that even their home is now lost and only his mother is left. With a vision that eludes even the telling of it, Cuthman sets out to build a cart in which he places his mother and leaves to find the place where he can work out his faith in God by building a church. In another play Christopher Fry describes the situation as follows.

Despite the protests of his mother, and they are constant and many, Cuthman pulls the cart to an unknown place which he expects God will reveal to him. When the willow strands that pull the cart break, he concludes, there he will partner with God to build the church.

"The church and I shall be built together; and together find our significance. Breaking and building in the progression of this world go hand in hand. And where the withies break I shall build."

And break they do and build he does, except for one final and fatal flaw in the plan. The work was almost done, and when suddenly a neighbor shouts, "The king-post has swung out of position!" Despite the labors of all and Cuthman's own desperate efforts, the post can not be moved into place and the building remains a skeleton that seemingly dies before it lives.

Suddenly, Cuthman appears running and shouting, "The king-post is in place again. The church will be finished!"

> "I was alone by the unattended pillar
> Mourning the bereaved air that lay so quiet
> Between walls; hungry for hammer blows.
> . . .
> But gradually I was aware of someone in
> The doorway and turned my eyes that way and saw
> Carved out of the sunlight a man who stood
> Watching me, so still that there was not
> Other such stillness anywhere on the earth.
> . . .
> He stretched his hand upon it. At his touch
> It lifted to its place. There was no sound.
> I cried out, and I cried at last "Who are You?"
> I heard him say "I was a carpenter" . . . [79]

The story of Cuthman is only a legend you say, that is true. But legend is one way of viewing truth with a 'slant,' as Emily Dickinson put it.

Tell all the truth, but tell it slant—

Success in Circuit lies
Too bright for our infirm Delight.
The Truth's superb surprise
As Lightning to the children eased
With explanation kind.
The Truth must dazzle gradually
Or every man be blind—[80]

While Cuthman had expanded his soul so as to capture the image of a church yet to be built, in the end he needed a companion of the soul to fulfill the vision. The truth in the legend is that Jesus of Nazareth grew up in a carpenter's home. He is the human form of God in the world, and after his resurrection, he moved through closed doors, and comes alongside of those who believe in him.

Cuthman put his heart and soul into the project he envisioned with faith, believing that God had inspired him. The human spirit by itself is capable of incredible faith and amazing feats; and it is thus that legends are born. We admire those who have the courage to struggle against impossible odds and those who refuse to accept defeat in the face of devastating losses. The spiritual nature of the human soul accounts for creative imagination in the face of bleak and colorless skies; the spiritual nature of the soul is the rising tide of faith following the retreat of the sea into the setting sun; the spiritual nature of the soul provides a grip for our hearts to grasp when we climb out of the dark night of the soul toward the dawn of a new season of hope.

We resonate with the ebb and flow of the human spirit through the seasons of our lives. And yet, there is another voice from one who has reached the summit, only to discover that the greatest of human success and achievement is, in the end, vanity. "Then I considered all that my hands had done and the toil I had spent in doing it, and again, all was vanity and a chasing after wind, and there was nothing to be gained under the sun" (Eccl. 2:9-

11).

The story of Cuthman takes us to the place where the soul stands amidst the ruins of its own finest creation and pauses in a silence heavy with despair. This story tells us that Jesus Christ stands alongside of our soul; he is not identical with our soul. And yet, by the Spirit the risen Christ enters into the space which our soul occupies in this world. The spiritual nature of the human soul is not that it can become 'Christ-like' but that it can recognize Christ who promises his Holy Spirit to us as the companion of our soul and to partner with our human spirit. "Abide in me as I abide in you," Jesus encouraged his disciples. "Apart from me, you can do nothing," (John 15:4,5). "I can do all things through him who strengthens me," wrote the apostle Paul (Phil. 4:13).

Jesus prepared the way for this by giving the promise of the Holy Spirit as a companion of the soul and to partner with us. Jesus promised that when he left and went to be with his Father, he would send the Holy Spirit to enter human souls through our personal response to him in relationship with God. "I will not leave you orphaned; I am coming to you" (John 14:18). Jesus spoke of the Spirit as "another counselor" who would stand with us and for us in our own spiritual journey (John 14:16). The Greek word *paraclete* can be translated as advocate, counselor or, even 'companion.' The word refers to one who stands alongside of another, acting as an encourager and one who empowers. Even as Jesus was their counselor and advocate during his time with them on earth, so he would return in the form of the Holy Spirit to partner with them as a spiritual companion.

Jesus believed in metaphors. They are one way of presenting truth 'with a slant!' The Bible is full of metaphors, as another way of speaking of truth. This is particularly the case when speaking of the ways in which God is experienced as a companion of the soul in creative partnership. "I am the vine, you are the branches,"

Jesus told his disciples (John 15:5). "I am the gate for the sheep," said Jesus on another occasion. "Whoever enters by me will be saved, and will come and go out and find pasture" (John 10:7, 9). King David too, sang his metaphors as poetry. "It is you who light my lamp; the Lord, my God, lights up my darkness. By you I can crush a troop, and by my God I can leap over a wall" (Ps 18:28-29). We have all had some walls which impede our progress or hem us in. The thought that God could give us a 'boost' over the wall is a compelling one!

In the story of Cuthman the 'king-post' may be seen as a metaphor which stands for that which connects the self, the world, and God. The 'king-post' holds body and soul together and anchors the self amidst the conflicts and chaos that sweeps across the landscape of life. The spirit which God breathed into the first humans can be one way of understanding the 'king-post.' As we shall see, this is held in place from our side by faith, as Cuthman attempted to do. But faith without being 'touched' from the side of God can also falter and fail.

Each person enters life with the 'king-post' out of alignment. The Bible speaks of this as the effects of sin, transmitted from our first parents in the Garden of Eden through each generation. Attempts to bring the self into alignment with God through our own efforts become a tower of Babel which never reaches heaven and only crumbles back down into the earth. Despite achieving a religious and moral life beyond his peers, the apostle Paul finally confessed that all this was but 'rubbish' when compared with the gift of new life through Jesus Christ which put into place the 'king-post' of his life (Philippians 3:4-11).

The metaphor of the 'king-post' is especially apt with respect to the soul because it represents that which ties together and holds together all of the component parts of a structure. When the soul attempts to do that alone by creating a center within the self, it ultimately faces frustration and defeat. In an earlier chapter I cited Emil Brunner who spoke of the 'sorrow of heart' which one ultimately experiences as a disharmony of existence when the self attempts to organize itself around its own center. God is not the 'king-post,' but rather the divine personal companion of the soul who comes to 'center' the self.

There is need of a center for the self which reaches back into the origins of the self within personal history and, at the same time, orients the contemporary self to a lodestar of future hope which shines its brightness into the darkest of days. Mary Vander Goot, using a different metaphor, puts it this way: "Today many people are longing for what now seems like an old-fashioned value, a cause, a goal, or an ideal that could be the lodestar of their lives. The emotional evidence of their predicament is their feeling of fragmentation. Their emotions seem to be like echoes without original sounds. They lack a center: they have no direction."[81]

When the 'king-post' of the soul is out of alignment, life becomes skewed and twisted. Nothing fits quite right. We may have success in achieving success in one area only to have another one slip out of our grasp. Lacking an anchor point which is seated in God, the soul is not earthquake resistant. It is like the house built on sand in the parable of Jesus, when the winds come it falls apart and is demolished (Matt. 7:24-27). When the 'king-post' is shaky, the soul needs to be 'retrofitted' by the divine carpenter! This is the work of the Spirit of God upon the soul, rather than a spiritual task given to the soul.

In this way we can think of God as the companion of the soul who partners with us in facing difficulties, overcoming failure and foolishness, and keeping alive the growing edge of life.

When King David was confronted by the prophet and had to admit that his life had spun out of control as the result of the unlawful taking for his own another man's wife and causing her husband's death, he sought and received restoration for his soul. In his prayer of confession to God he wrote, "Against you and you alone have I sinned. . . Create in me a clean heart, O God and put a new right spirit within me" (Psalm 51:4, 10).

When the 'king-post' of his soul has been put right by the divine companion, David expresses himself in this way: "I keep the Lord always before me; because he is at my right hand, I shall not be moved. Therefore my heart is glad, and my soul rejoices; my body also rests secure ...You show me the path of life. In your presence there is fullness of joy; in your right hand are pleasures forevermore" (Psalms 16:8-11).

The creative partnering between the soul and God is able to transform the barren places in our lives into gardens of beauty and bounty. "The wilderness and the dry land shall be glad, the dessert shall rejoice and blossom ... For waters shall break forth in the wilderness, and streams in the desert," sings the prophet in anticipation of divine creativity let loose upon the field of humanity. (Isaiah 35:1, 6). The creative partnering between the soul and God can transform fear and anxiety into courage and peace. "Say to those who are of a fearful heart, 'Be strong, do not fear! Here is your God'" (Isaiah 35:4).

What really then holds the 'king-post' of the soul in place? What is it that gives the soul a center which cannot be moved, but which does not move except aroused and stirred to action by a compelling presence that touches the core of our being? The 'king-post' is held in place by faith. Not blind faith which stares into the void until an apparition appears of our own making. Not foolish faith which flexes its muscles and flaunts its courage in the absence of evidence. Not nervous faith which darts back and forth like a sparrow approaching a crumb of bread too close to a human foot.

What kind of faith did Cuthman have? As a young shepherd boy, he used faith like a child might play at magic.

"It might have been because my stomach was empty," he acknowledges, "That I was suddenly filled with faith—suddenly parcelled with faith like a little wain." Taking a stick, he drew a circle around his sheep saying, "God guard them here...though as a fence I knew it was less good than a bubble." Going off to dinner, he returned to find that they had eaten up to he very edge of the invisible circle, but not beyond. You see, he exclaimed, "God guards them!" After being told that his father had died, he cries out cries out in anguish, "Did I steal God away from my father to guard my sheep?"

When the sun is warm upon our shoulders and the wind is at our back, faith rises within us with the dawn of a new day. But the sunlit vision of faith can quickly turn into a dark nightmare of doubt and despair when the storm clouds appear to hide the face of God.

> How is your faith now, Cuthman? . . .
> Is God still in the air
> Now that the sun is down?
> They are afraid in the city,
> Sleepless in the town.
> Cold on the roads,
> Desperate by the river.
> Can faith for long elude
> Prevailing fever?

Later, with a vision of building a cart and traveling to another place to build a church, he says, "I have stayed too long with the children, a boy sliding on the easy ice, skating the foolish silver... Even as I have been faithful in the green recklessness of little knowledge, Grant this O God, that I may grow to my father as he grew to Thy son, and be his son now and for always."[82]

Faith, however, cannot serve as the 'king-post' of the soul until it is set in place by its object—the reality of God upon whom the soul depends for its very existence.

The Companion of the Soul

For Cuthman, as we have seen, the story drew near a dreadful climax. Despite his legendary faith manufactured out of deep grief and persistent piety, the 'king-post' of his faith faltered and failed. Perhaps he would have become a legend even then, but not a saint. He would have been remembered both as evidence of fanatical faith and also as a warning to others.

In the end, his faith was restored, not by his own efforts nor even by his desperate plight, but by an approach of a heavenly figure with a carpenter's hands. Tell it true, but tell it slant, lest it dazzle and make us blind. There would be no church without a Cuthman; there would be no garden without a gardener. For all of the human soul's creative imagination, for all of God's creative power, the two must partner to accomplish earthly tasks that have eternal significance.

The woman's face on the television screen was a tormented image of silent despair and grief. Her two young children had died in the bombing of the federal building in Oklahoma City early in 1995. Silently weeping, clutching two teddy bears, the camera captured the pathetic image at the nationally televised memorial service.

Some weeks later, in response to a reporter's question as to how she managed to face life with hope and optimism following the loss, she replied: "It is my faith that keeps me going," she responded. "Without faith in God I don't know how I could live through this loss and rebuild my life." When this same woman some months later had a surgical operation allowing her to conceive again so that she might have other children, television reporters called it a "miracle of faith."

The reporter's comment was not prompted by the surgery that reversed a previous tubal ligation. It was her vision of having more children, reuniting with her estranged husband, and the beginning of a new life that evoked the response, "a miracle of faith." The medical marvel is a product of technology and science. The human spirit is not so easily re-manufactured when it has been broken.

We cannot help but admire persons who survive difficult ordeals without collapsing into self-pity and bitterness. How does one achieve this kind of faith in the face of adversity and tragic loss? Is faith a spiritual gift to the chosen few, or is it a resource which each one of us has at our disposal if only we could find the key?

It was a desperate father who first uttered the words, "I believe; help my unbelief!" When the disciples failed to heal his son, he turned to Jesus with a cautious request, "If you are able to do anything, have pity on us and help us."

"If you are able! —All things can be done for the one who believes," replied Jesus. The mild rebuke was coupled with a challenge and promise. Faith born of desperation may not be pure, but it is persistent.

"I believe; help my unbelief," was the father's tortured reply (Mark 9:22-24). As much as he loved his son and longed for his healing, could he really be sure that his faith did not have a fatal flaw of doubt. Could any of us be certain?

The boy was healed. As for the father, was his request granted because he had sufficient faith despite his disclaimer, or because his desperation overcame his doubt? Part of faith is knowing that it is not our faith but the one in whom we put our trust that turns the key. The test of faith is the capacity to believe when there are no visible evidences on which to rely. It is not the absence of evidences which evokes faith; it is just that some of the evidences on which faith rests are invisible, though real.

For all of the holy terror of the sanctuary, a confession of faith, as some have discovered, is easier to make than the long term living out of faith. Facing life out in the world can sometimes be more difficult than facing God in the sanctuary.

Faith at work is apparently more pleasing to God than faith at rest. The profession of faith is fine, wrote James, but what good is it without works? "Even the demons believe," James reminded his readers. For James, faith that didn't work was of no practical value. While others made great claims to faith, James countered, "By my works I will show you my faith" (James 2:18-19).

In his highly acclaimed book, *The Seat of the Soul*, Gary Zukav presents his version of New Age spirituality. While he talks about reverence, trust, and even prayer, there is no mention of faith. In the vocabulary of new age thought there is no personal God, no personal Spirit of God, no companion to the soul in its spiritual journey. In place of God there is a vague and impersonal concept of Divine Intelligence, or Light, which infuses the soul so as to make the soul itself divine. The 'teacher' which directs the soul is also impersonal, and does not actually interact with the soul as personal being. "Think of what you are doing as entering into partnership with Divine Intelligence," Zukav writes, "a partnership in which you begin to share your concerns with the understanding that there is an Intelligence receptive to what you are saying that helps you create within your own environment of matter and energy the most effective dynamics to bring you into wholeness."[83] Here, Zukav appears to be using the soul as a metaphor which has no objective reality as its ground. This is a 'slant' that does not reveal all of the truth.

In New Age spirituality each individual soul is a separate incarnation of soul itself, and the spiritual life of the soul is essentially a solitary one. Interaction with Divine Intelligence may be called partnership but it is not companionship. Partners share a common task while each remains a solitary self. Companions share a common life experience which makes the task of each a communion of souls.

I like the slant put on the truth by the story of

Cuthman.

>He stretched his hand upon it. At his touch
>It lifted to its place. There was no sound.
>I cried out, and I cried at last "Who are You?"
>I heard him say "I was a carpenter" . . .

The journey of the human soul is an earthly one, but not a lonely one. The Creator God has been a companion on that journey from the childlike innocence of the Garden of Eden to the troubled and tangled pathways of our lost childhood. Perhaps we have not experienced the touch of the carpenter's hand upon our soul until we lean against the 'king-post' with all of our might. Faith may be found at last, when we least need it to save our honor, but when we can most likely use it to heal our hearts. Perhaps we too shall be a saint, if not a legend!

EIGHT

The Healing of the Soul: Recovering From Deep Injuries to the Soul

We are born broken. We live by mending.
The grace of God is the glue. (Eugene O'Neil)[84]

I was in my teens, as I remember the incident, sitting on the edge of the family circle nursing some grievance, the source of which escapes me now. When someone commented on my lack of participation, my mother responded, "Don't mind Ray, he's just got his feelings hurt!"

As I recall, the remark did not have a therapeutic effect! It was a common enough expression in those days, and I suppose that suffering attributed to hurt feelings was thought to be like the common cold—there was no cure for it, but we were expected to get over it in a few days.

In retrospect, the reference to hurt feelings is a curious expression. What are feelings and how can they be hurt? One feels pain when injured, and when the doctor applies pressure to a sore spot on the body, we say "it hurts." The days of our childhood are filled with flurries of feelings, most of which seem to disappear without a trace, like a frown which suffers a meltdown in the face of a smile. But there are feelings in every child, that hurt beyond the telling. These painful feelings can become lodged in the membrane of the soul like painful tumors, which refuse to be healed and hurt again with each new bruise.

When my feelings are hurt, I hurt from the inside out. There is no scrape on the knee or cut on the finger to which I can point when someone says, "Let me kiss it and make it feel better!" When my soul is wounded I know that no one else in all the world feels as terrible as I do. I feel the cut, the stab and the stinging pain. The throb of hurt feelings is impervious to the analgesic remedies offered by well-meaning persons who seek to cheer me up!

"Just leave him alone," they say, when we won't dance at their party or join their parade. "He'll join us when he feels like it." They don't realize that if we have been hurt, injury has been done to us. We have been wounded. We can't just forget about it. We feel violated because the core of the soul has been trampled on. Feelings are not merely emotions lodged in the psychological self, but responses coming from the moral and spiritual nature of the soul.

The New Age writer, Gary Zukav, has a quite different explanation. He locates feelings in the personality but not in the soul. "The fearful and violent emotions that have come to characterize human existence can be experienced only by the personality. Only the personality can feel anger, fear, vengeance, sorrow, shame, regret, indifference, frustration, cynicism and loneliness. . . but love, compassion, and wisdom do not come from the personality. They are experiences of the soul."[85] Does this mean that the soul itself is not wounded and in need of healing? If so, then the soul becomes the healer by resolving the feelings of the personality into a deeper wisdom of the immortal soul. Whatever moral judgments arise within the self, Zukav dismisses as merely the judgmental nature of the personality, having no objective validity. The task of the soul is to neutralize moral judgments, not to authenticate them.

In contrast, a biblical view of the soul locates the feelings of moral outrage against conditions and actions which violate the dignity of the self in the spiritual nature of the soul. Jesus often expressed strong emotions of anger and outrage against the effects of disease and evil actions of others as equivalent to God's own moral judgment. For example, when confronted with the devastating effects of leprosy in a person asking for healing, the Scripture says, "Moved with pity, Jesus stretched out his hand and touched him. . . Immediately the leprosy left him, and he was made clean" (Mark 1:40-42). Some manuscript versions of this passage from Mark use the word 'anger' rather than 'pity.' This would be in accord with other references to Jesus' feelings of anger. When the religious authorities accused him of breaking the law of God on the sabbath by healing a man, Mark records, "He looked around them with anger; he was grieved at their hardness of heart" (Mark 3:5).

Many Scripture texts portray the strong feelings of Jesus as responses from the core of his very being, that is, from his soul. Early in his ministry he reacted with strong feelings against the violation of the temple by those who used it for profit in exchanging money and selling animals. "Making a whip of cords, he drove all of them out of the temple, both the sheep and the cattle. He also poured out the coins of the money changers and overturned their tables. He told those who were selling the doves, 'Take these things out of here! Stop making my Father's house a marketplace!'" (John 2:15,16). In facing his own impending suffering and death on the cross, Jesus cried out: "Now my soul is troubled" (John 12:27). The author of the book of Hebrews tells us, "In the days of his flesh, Jesus offered up prayers and supplications, with loud cries and tears, to the one who was able to save him from death, and he was heard because of his reverent submission" (Hebrews 5:7).

Are we to account for these strong emotions and expressions of moral outrage on the part of Jesus simply to 'bad karma' which was lodged in his personality?

Hardly. He acts as our 'priest,' the scripture tells us, "who in every respect has been tested as we are" (Hebrews 4:15). The healing of deep injuries to our own souls is a therapy of moral and spiritual renewal on the part of God's own 'priestly soul' which touches us with love and compassion. Such healing is much more than resolution of psychological conflicts in the personality.

The wounds to the soul are laced with moral feelings, which often can result in a sense of deep shame at the core of our being, and loss of self-esteem. Not all injuries to the soul cause long term damage to the self. There are some injuries which heal with time. These can be painful but need not be permanent. Recovery from injuries produced by violation of our deepest feelings at the core of the soul, however, require moral resolution in addition to emotional repair. These are injuries to the soul which are experienced as violations of one's self, both physical and personal. When these kind of injuries occur in childhood, the hurt may be carried into adulthood. Recognition of the moral violation incurred in these type of injuries is necessary to the healing of the soul and its recovery of health.

When small children become involved in conflict over possession of a toy, and one bites or pulls the hair of the other when robbed of the toy, we witness moral outrage in a very primitive form. When a child feels violated, the typical reaction is to resort to some form of violence against the offender. What lies concealed in this reaction is the deeper moral injury done to the one whose toy was taken, or whose personal sense of self was violated. When a child expresses moral outrage in some form of violent behavior, the offended child now becomes an offender, and is made to feel guilty. To force a child prematurely to say, "I am sorry," compounds the feelings of moral outrage. One cannot really "feel sorry" for the anger which becomes an authentic expression of moral outrage. Only when the sense of moral outrage is dealt with can the feelings of anger subside so that forgiveness can be offered and received.

Moral instincts are found in every child, says Psychotherapist W. W. Meissner. "We violate children and arouse them to an inner rage when we keep them from the guidance and support they need to develop fully."[86] Children, of course, have not yet developed a category of moral discrimination. Their actions, while not expressed in moral terms, are grounded in a sense of moral outrage. This moral outrage is often blind and out of control. Nonetheless, it is an expression of a wounded soul.

Moral injuries are not healed in the same way as other injuries to the soul. Rather, these injuries must be treated as violations of one's innate sense of moral dignity and personhood. Recovery begins when the deeper moral outrage is acknowledged and the core self is affirmed as basically good, even though the behavior resulting from the outrage is not acceptable. This is impossible for the morally wounded soul to do alone. If the soul itself is injured and experiences moral outrage, it cannot heal itself, for the soul cannot pass moral judgment upon its own actions. If it does, it results in shame and loss of personal worth rather than healing.

This is why the concept of the soul as the healer of the personality as offered by Gary Zukav is inadequate. First, in his view, the soul is not the seat of moral agency and thus does not suffer moral injury when there is a violation of the core self. Second, the soul works on its task of discharging the debt of karma alone, with only a 'guide' and 'teacher' to assist, both of which are impersonal. In this version of the soul, healing is achieved by moving beyond the five senses of external power into the 'higher self' which has access to inner power infused with divine Intelligence. In effect, this is a 'spiritual healing' without addressing the moral injury to the soul itself. The expression of moral outrage is explained by the soul as an inappropriate expression of the personality, but not to be judged as wrong. This has the effect of repressing moral outrage rather than validating and healing it.

Moral outrage which is not permitted to be expressed honestly and openly can often be deflected back upon the soul as shame and self-condemnation. Shame is a loss of moral worth and power. The injury inflicted upon the soul when moral outrage is not recognized and resolved is the negative feeling of shame. In exploring the effect of shame upon the soul, we come closer to recovering from deep injuries to the soul.

As God's children, Adam and Eve are endowed with the divine image and likeness which is an innate sense of moral worth and value. As they are open and supportive of each other's integrity and worth, the story says that they were "both naked, and were not ashamed." When they experience the violation of that inner sense of value through the misleading guidance of the serpent, and eat the forbidden fruit, they now feel shame as a loss of personal worth. They flee from the presence of God, cover themselves with fig leaves, and seek a place of concealment amidst the trees in the garden. The healing power of God uncovers their sense of shame and moral confusion (Genesis 2:25; 3:8-21). While there are consequences of their actions which each must accept, the judgment of God reveals moral failure (sin) and restores moral empowerment (grace). In receiving grace, they receive more than mercy. The metaphor of clothing which God provides is a gracious sign that they are accepted and valued as the children of God that they essentially are.

Shame has to do with feeling a loss to one's identity and worth as well as acknowledging guilt for wrong doing. When I feel guilt in the circumstance of having broken a traffic law, I may often continue to feel shame long after the ticket has been paid. I experience a loss of personal integrity. My self-worth is threatened. Paying the traffic ticket removes the guilt, but does not restore my sense of personal worth. Long after the guilt has been removed objectively, one can still be caught in the dehumanizing grip of shame.

Shame is like a spreading stain which seeps into hidden recesses in the self. Shame does not necessarily disappear even though guilt as an objective offense standing between God and human persons is removed. Shame, as the deeper problem of the soul, means that one has suffered loss of worth, not merely loss of status. The purpose of divine forgiveness is not only to pardon sin as a legal or objective fault, but also to overcome and cleanse the shame which has weakened and stained the inner fabric of the soul. The power of shame is only broken when we are empowered by a new sense of moral and personal worth.

We realize that not all feelings of shame are so destructive to the self. Indeed, the capacity to feel shame seems to be part of the self's maintenance of a healthy sense of limitation and even the core of humility. To be called "shameless" is to judged to be without a sense of discrimination as to what is appropriate and what is inappropriate behavior.

"In the past the capacity to experience shame was valued," says Robert Karen. "To be capable of shame meant to be modest, as opposed to exhibitionistic or grandiose, to have character, nobility, honor, discretion. It meant to be respectful of social standards, of the boundaries of others, of one's own limitations. And, finally, it meant to be respectful of one's need for privacy."[87]

The capacity for shame has a spiritual basis and is grounded in the soul, not merely as a negative component of the personality. To have a sense of shame is akin to feeling God's presence.[88] A capacity for shame is a mark of the human soul's awareness of divine presence.

The restoration of personal being and the recovery

of a sense of self-worth is a process of restoration through communication and community. Shame isolates; recovery must restore relation. Shame causes inner rage and fury against the self; recovery must disarm that abusive emotion. Shame eats away at the tender and vulnerable core of the soul turning healthy self love into ritual abuse. Toxic shame is the pervasive corrosion of the soul through emotional self-abuse.[89]

Recovery must stop the self-abuse of shame and release the power of forgiveness and healing into the innermost cell of the life of the soul. To be shame-based, is not only to experience a deep sense of personal deficit but also to experience oneself as caught in a web of shame that conceals a secret. This secret may lie hidden in one's family of origin. In many families, shame is carried from one generation to another, long after the incident which caused the shame has been forgotten. The secret which led to the original shame dies with a previous generation while the shame continues to be hidden, passed from one generation to the next.

Shame can be transmitted from one generation to another as individuals in the family acquire a sense of unworthiness or inadequacy. This may be disguised as feelings of racial inferiority, social unacceptability, or gender deficiency. In many families and entire societies, women are led to feel inferior or inadequate due to their biological nature and gender-assigned roles. These are all ways of transmitting shame from one generation to another.

Gary Zukav would call this evidence of the 'karma debt' which the soul acquires in its most recent incarnation in a specific human personality. The task of the soul is to nullify this 'bad karma' and through wisdom receive compassion and love as healing for the personality. In his view, healing is the work of the soul digging out the feelings in the personality which lie behind shame, thus discharging the 'karma debt' inherited from a previous in-

The Healing of the Soul

carnation.

In an earlier chapter I discussed the way in which the soul of each of us is related to the soul of the communities in which we are born and which provide early experiences of nurture and development. It is the soul, not merely the personality which feels moral outrage, shame and loss of self-esteem. The intergenerational nature of these feelings reside in the social, if not the biological, structure of each person's life. Each child is born with a capacity for shame. Each of us is dependent upon the physical, emotional and spiritual care provided by the primary community for the grace, love and moral empowerment to heal the soul from feelings of actual shame and guilt. When the soul of the community is itself the repository of ancient evil, hidden shame, and negative self worth, each soul in that community will bear its share. Robert Bellah speaks of this as the 'memory' of a community which has "painful stories of shared suffering as well as shared love; it will remember not only stories of suffering received but of suffering inflicted—dangerous memories, for they call the community to alter ancient evils."[90]

The corrosive effect of shame in the soul leads to the erosion of the capacity to esteem the self.[91] Lack of healthy self-worth is not merely a deficit to the soul, but it also can take the form of a more insidious self-hate.[92] Positive self-worth may be defined as the absence of self-hate. Is self-hate too strong a term? Most of us do not like to think that we actually hate ourselves. Yet, most of us would admit to times when we have said to ourselves, if not to others, "I hate myself when I do things like that." Even as we say it, we are probably using the words as a form of self-scolding. We really mean that we hate the things that we do. But the message seeps through to the core of shame in the soul nonetheless and reinforces negative self-worth.

Recovery from deep injuries to the soul is a process

of healing which involves recognition and authentication of the moral outrage which results from violation of personal dignity and integrity. This usually is complicated by the fact that moral outrage as I have shown, often results in inappropriate responses and behavior which cause us to be the offender as well as the offended one. We continue in a cycle of guilt and shame. Because this is an injury to the soul and not merely a personality conflict caused by 'bad karma,' the soul itself must be affirmed as morally good and absolved of moral wrong through grace and forgiveness. The Bible is clear and compelling in its affirmation of the essential moral good of the human soul as created in God's image and likeness, as well as in confronting the human soul with its sin against the Creator and the loss of moral rectitude. Recovery of the soul from both shame and loss of self-worth is achieved when the soul receives blessing rather than condemnation

The biblical concept of blessing was meant to empower the self with a sense of worth and value. Shame produces what some psychologists have called a 'narcissistic injury' to the self. The self-love which is a God-created image in the human self through which we seek fulfillment and pleasure, is crushed and crippled by shame. In our desperate search for happiness we cry out for rights and benefits when we what we really need is blessing.

When Jacob fled from his brother Esau, after conspiring to rob him of the birthright, he was in a state of turmoil and uncertainty. He had acquired the birthright but had not gained the blessing of inner peace. What appeared to be flight from the only place that he had known and the only family that he had, dysfunctional as it was, turned out to be a pilgrimage to promise. Falling asleep in the wilderness, with a stone for a pillow, he dreamed of angels ascending and descending on a ladder that reached into heaven. Awakening, he cried out: "Surely the Lord is in this place—and I did not know it!"

(Gen. 28:16). The hard stone of shame became a ladder of blessing through a vision of God's grace in his life.

Jacob set up the stone as an altar to God, naming the place Bethel—house of God. While this marked the spot where he made the discovery as a religious shrine, the greater significance was the discovery deep within himself that he was really blessed by God. Up to that time he no doubt felt shame at the means used to secure the birthright at the expense of his brother Esau. Whatever the damage done to that relationship and the guilt incurred it was nothing compared to the shame which ate away in his soul.

Jacob's discovery was the internalizing of the blessing which now came directly from God's own word. He arrived at the place under the burden of shame, and left with the blessing of his soul healing. Now he has the blessing, and the shame is gone, with its power of self-condemnation.[93] He is free to move into relationship with his brother Esau and to make restitution for the wrong done to him.

There is a blessing for us when the hard stone of crushing shame and self condemnation can be turned into a ladder with angels carrying manna from heaven to feed our starving souls! It is wise for us as well to have an outward point of reference for the inner experience of blessing. Bethel marks the place of discovery and the beginning of recovery. There is freedom to continue the journey knowing that the blessing is abiding in our souls and the stone remains to mark the place.[94]

The feeling of being blessed can only be described, but it cannot be defined. It is something that one must experience. It cannot be taught but it can be learned. There is no technique by which it can be achieved, but there is a pathway that leads toward it. It is more discovery than discipline.

When Jesus exhorted us to "receive the kingdom of God as a little child," it is an encouragement to rediscover the longing which opens us up to God's love and the fulfillment of the self in another (Matt. 18:3) It may well be that Jesus was reminding adults that they carry within them a child-like longing which is the spiritual core of the soul. This child-like joy and happiness is the motivating source for self-fulfillment that is indispensable to faith, hope and love. The self-love which is typical of the child is a form of self-pleasure at its most elemental level. The love of God is an empowering love, aimed at evoking in each person the desire for the kingdom of God and "everything else added to it" (Matt. 6:33). God's desire is to give us all things that pertain to life and happiness.

The recovery of the soul from deep injuries and the restoration of positive self-worth results from an empowering experience of unconditional acceptance and love through which the original capacity for self-pleasure and self-fulfillment can be restored in a healthy way. The beginning of spiritual healing appears in the encounter with another self. This is a healing encounter, for it is one which creates wholeness out of what had only been a part. We must not pass too quickly over this momentous moment. The recovery of the soul does not occur by transcending the "flesh and bones," of our physical existence, but through the encounter of the soul of the other through one's own embodied existence.

The biblical concept of the image of God is grounded in the experience of the self with others. While each person is fully endowed with the image of God, this divine image is experienced in the self's encounter with others. In this depiction of the formation of the first humans there is an empowerment to discover and experience the being of one with and through the other.[95]

The other person provides the necessary boundary for the self to be experienced in a relation of mutual trust and acceptance. Recovery of the soul does not come though the healing of emotional pain alone. True recovery means the discovery of one's own moral and spiritual self as affirmed by God and empowered through divine love and grace. Our souls are vulnerable, and they need to be nourished with care!

NINE

The Care of the Soul: A Guide to Spiritual Fitness

If the focus of the twentieth century has been on outer space, the focus of the twenty-first century may well be on inner space. (George Gallop)[96]

"Take care," my friend said, as he turned and walked away after our lunch meeting, without waiting for a response. I reflected for a few minutes on what has become a casual ritual of parting. If I had asked him how he thought I should do this, I would probably have embarrassed him by demanding more than he intended to say. On the other hand, I would probably have been uncomfortable if he said more than I wanted to hear!

"You need to take better care of your health," says the medical doctor, as she writes a prescription for reducing elevated blood pressure. "You need to take more care about what you eat," warns the nutritionist as he submits a list of "good and bad" foods. "You need to take care to lower your level of stress," advises the psychologist, as she outlines a program of relaxation techniques. "You need to take better care of your body," urges the physical fitness trainer, as he develops a personal plan for increasing muscle tone and decreasing body fat.

Fitness is in. Flabbiness is out. Apparently that applies to the soul as well. Spiritual fitness is something that more and more people are caring about.

Thomas Moore's best selling book, *Care of the Soul*, published in 1992, spoke to a growing concern for a spirituality of the inner life. Other books quickly followed, some from a more overtly religious perspective.[97]

In reading the current literature on care of the soul, three themes keep emerging as evidence of the need for soul care. In our contemporary culture, the soul is often described as *undernourished*, *overburdened*, and *disconnected*. To the extent that this is true, we may be one of the most religious societies in all of the world, but also the most spiritually unfit. In this chapter I want to examine each of these three areas of the life of the soul and provide some guidelines for spiritual fitness.

First, if our souls are undernourished it may be because a great deal of popular religion is of the 'fast food' variety, highly seasoned, easily accessible and in disposable containers, requiring no preparation and little interruption of our fast-paced daily life. Purveyors of fast food have learned that people tend to prefer what is tasty rather than what is nourishing. Both the religious world and the secular world have now caught on. The daily life of the self is filled to excess while the soul is starving. Part of spiritual fitness is the re-education of our taste, so that an appetite can be developed for that which is nourishing for the soul.

The signs of an undernourished soul can take many forms. Bruce Demarest suggests that the undernourished soul can suffer intellectually when asked to thrive only on thoughts rather than on feelings. Or, the soul can suffer emotional deadness due to lack of strong affect such as compassion, grief, joy, or even anger. The undernourished soul can suffer relationally when the outer life becomes driven more by task and function than by communion with fellow souls.[98]

Lack of nourishment for the soul is a comparison Jesus was making when he asked: "Is there anyone among you who, if your child asks for bread, will give a stone?" (Matthew 7:9) We all know the difference between bread and stones when it comes to physical food. Soul hunger and soul food, however are not so easily recognized. When our inner self becomes emaciated it may not be due to lack of quantity, but of quality. People are known to have died of malnutrition while consuming large amounts of food with little or no nutritional content. Some nourishment for the soul, however, may not depend so much on the kind of food but how it is offered and received. The undernourished soul may lack a connection as much as calories.

When the soul 'flutters its wings,' it is asking for more than food. Let me explain.

Sitting in a chair on the walkway outside the local Donut Hut, drinking my coffee on a morning break from writing, I observed the sparrows darting around picking up crumbs. They became quite bold, as each rushed to pick up crumbs from around my feet. It was not just that I was a messy eater, but dropping a few crumbs intentionally provided diversion and entertainment. Each sparrow fiercely fought to get to the crumbs—no sharing among their peers! Then, as I watched, one smaller sparrow made no attempt to pick a crumb, but simply fluttered its wings ever so slightly. A nearby sparrow hopped over and offered the bit of food from its own mouth directly to the mouth of the smaller sparrow. I assumed that this was the baby sparrow continuing to look to its mother for food. The size of the two sparrows appeared insignificant, as the smaller one looked quite capable of picking up crumbs for itself. The little flutter of its wings, however, was the signal which brought the mother hopping over for the feeding.

As I watched, I wondered at what point the smaller sparrow would have to pick its own crumbs and compete with the others, rather than being fed mouth-to-mouth. My guess is that the time was rapidly approaching and probably long past when this should happen. The smaller sparrow had a good thing going! As long as it made no attempt to pick its own crumbs and made the familiar gesture with the fluttering wings, it received its nourishment. Surely the smaller sparrow was reaching out for care more than for crumbs. Too often, I fear, we give our soul crumbs when we should be seeking care. Each of us can find crumbs, but do crumbs truly nourish our souls? "One does not live by bread alone," Jesus said, " but by every word that comes from the mouth of God" (Matthew 4:4).

Our soul is the child within us, requiring the nourishment of loving care. The soul thrives on care rather than on competition. The soul develops and matures but never outgrows its need to be fed. The soul's appetite can only be nourished by that which satisfies the craving of the spirit for truths which are imperishable. These truths pass from the 'lips of God,' as it were, directly to the deep need of the soul.

Some believe in a spiritual discipline which demands regular time set aside for reading the Bible. While this can be helpful, unless the soul delights in the Word of God, an imposed discipline may be more like a stone than bread for the soul. Even what passes for a 'Bible study group' can end up more like sparrows competing for crumbs than hungry souls fluttering their wings. Can it be that many souls are suffering from malnutrition even while being stuffed with biblical texts. How can the soul thrive when it has no appetite for what nourishes its spiritual core? What if the stories and texts of the Bible were approached with the same intensity with which we long for and devour letters from a loved one?

Spiritual fitness begins with a healthy appetite. The desire of the soul for comfort is the craving for God's love which satisfies. The Psalmist expresses craving for the words and precepts of God: "How sweet are your words to my taste, sweeter than honey to my mouth"(Psalms 119:103)! "The precepts of the Lord are right," sings the Psalmist, "rejoicing the heart. . . More to be desired are they than gold, even much fine gold; sweeter also than honey, and drippings of the honeycomb" (Psalms 19:8-11).

Perhaps we have made a mistake when we substitute the word 'Bible,' which is only a language symbol, for what is actually the 'Word of God.' Even 'Holy Scripture' does not arouse much of an appetite when it is overlade with symbols of religiosity. The Psalmist says, "how sweet are your words," not, "how much I reverence the book!" The soul knows the difference between bread and stone. And the soul seeks the care behind the words as much as the words themselves.

Job suffered incredible pain and anguish despite the torrent of words his friends offered as good counsel. What he longed for, however, was not sacred texts and pious platitudes, but some intimation that his Creator God was aware of his situation, cared for him, and would speak words in his defense. Job was fluttering the wings of his soul, waiting for words straight from the mouth of God. "If mortals die, will they live again? All the days of my service I would wait until my release should come. You would call, and I would answer you; you would long for the work of your hands" (Job 14:14,15). When the words came at last, even though carrying a mild rebuke, Job was satisfied. "I had heard of you by the hearing of the ear, but now my eye sees you" (Job 42:5).

My father was not a man given to pious talk and, as a good Lutheran, wore his faith inconspicuously but close to his heart. In retrospect, as I think of his life, I think of a man with a well nourished soul, capable of withstanding crop failures and finally cancer, without blaming God or cursing his own misfortune. Whatever Biblical texts he learned were in the Norwegian language in preparation for the ritual of confirmation. When English replaced Norwegian in the home, and became the 'mother tongue' in which I was confirmed, my father made the transition without skipping a heartbeat of faith in his soul.

On his deathbed, when we finally were unable to rouse any response through our own words and he sank into a deep coma, we concluded that the window to his soul had closed. When the Pastor came, however, and standing by his side began to recite the words of Psalm 23, "The Lord is my shepherd . . . ," my father moved his hands from his side and folded them across his chest. That was the first and last movement he made during the last few hours of his life on earth. Invisible to us, my father's soul was fluttering its wings, and the sweet Word of God found its way directly to him, gently nourishing his soul.

We attend to the hearing of the Word of God, meditate upon it, and open our souls in worship filled with wonder, adoration and praise as a way of acquiring a taste and craving for that which nourishes us in life and satisfies us in death. We may experience frailty and even disability of the body and yet experience spiritual fitness as we are nourished by words that God speaks directly to our souls.

Giving attention to the care and nourishment of our souls is something akin to what Douglas Webster calls 'soulcraft.' Using the analogy of carpentry, which is the art of cutting, working, and joining timber into a structure, he defines soulcraft as "the art of discerning, applying and enjoying the wisdom of God in every aspect of life. . . . It is an eternal work right at the heart of everyday, ordinary life. It restores the rhythms of grace to the routines of life and inspires us to live today in the light of eternity."[99]

I have suggested that in our contemporary culture our souls may often be undernourished. They can also be overburdened. Even the strongest soul can bend beneath burdens that are unnecessary. Spiritual fitness is not determined by how heavy a burden may be borne in life, but how well we bear the burdens that are necessary and how easily we let go of the ones that are not. The invitation of Jesus was not a promise to free us from all burdens, but to 'fit' our burden to our souls. "Come to me, all you that are weary and are carrying heavy burdens, and I will give you rest. Take my yoke upon you, and learn from me; for I am gentle and humble in heart, and you will find rest for your souls. For my yoke is easy, and my burden is light" (Matthew 11:28-30).

A soul without a burden is immature and irresponsible. There are burdens that only we can bear, and there are burdens that can only be borne in being yoked to another. The apostle Paul has this in mind when he wrote: "Bear one another's burdens, and in this way you will fulfill the law of Christ. For if those who are nothing think they are something, they deceive themselves. All must test their own work; then that work, rather than their neighbor's work, will become a cause for pride. For all must carry their own loads" (Galatians 6:2-5). When we "bear one another's burden," we acknowledge to ourselves and to others that there are burdens that simply cannot be borne alone. At the same time, "all must carry their own load," for there are burdens that no one else can bear for us.

When we end up overburdened in life, we fall into the fallacy of thinking that we can control our lives. If we could just take on one more task, do one more thing for others, work harder on getting our own life in shape, then we could prevent the looming chaos from overtaking us and make everything come out just right. The fallacy is exposed by Jesus' rhetorical question, "which of you by anxious care, can add a single hour to your span of life? If then you are not able to do so small a thing as that, why do you worry about the rest?" (Luke 12:25,26)

Even the lightest burden will break us if borne for the wrong reason. The burden that only we can bear has nothing to do with controlling our life and making everything work out. The burden that each of has is to 'flutter' our own wings, like the little sparrow who receives nourishment because it asks for it. This is the burden of faith, the burden of hope and the burden of love.

The Hebrew psalmist put this philosophy of life in poetic form.

> May those who sow in tears reap with
>   shouts of joy.
>   Those who go out weeping,
>   bearing the seed for sowing,
>   shall come home with shouts of joy,
>   carrying their sheaves. (Psalm 126)

A literal translation of the Hebrew reads this way:

> He surely toils along weeping,
> carrying the burden of seed;
> he surely comes in with rejoicing,
> carrying his sheaves.

The burden of hope can only be borne through the practical power of faith. Let me suggest some ways in which faith carries the burden of hope.

First, the burden of hope is the anguish over what has already been lost. In the poignant sonnet by Edna St. Vincent Millay, it is with "twisted face" that the man with the pocket full of seeds moves toward the future. We should never forget this. The burden of hope always emerges out of the ruins of some failed dream, some unfulfilled desire, some loss that must be grieved.

> The broken dike, the levee washed away,
> The good fields flooded and the cattle drowned,
> Estranged and treacherous all the faithful
>   ground,

> And nothing left but bloating disarray
> Of tree and home uprooted... was this the day
> Man dropped upon his shadow without a sound
> And died, having laboured well and having found
> His burden heavier than a quilt of clay?
> No, no, I saw him when the sun had set
> In water, leaning on his single oar
> Above his garden faintly glimmering yet...
> There bulked the plough, here washed the updrifted weeds...
> And scull across his roof and make for shore,
> With twisted face and pocket full of seeds.[100]

If there is a kind of hope that carries no burden, it is childish and immature. It is short-term and short-lived. It flickers brightly for an instant and then just as quickly dissolves with the first tears of frustration over the loss of some simple pleasure. Hope requires risk, so much that it hurts. Hope makes us vulnerable to fragile plans of future dreams and even greater loss. Hope exposes us to disappointment, frustration and betrayal. Faith plants the seed and promises a harvest, and so creates hope. But with the promise of a harvest comes the possibility that the promise will fail. That is the betrayal that hope must bear. Without faith as the investment of one's precious life and resources in the power of life, the burden of hope could not be borne. But faith bears that burden in partnership with hope, for it is partnership with God, the author and creator of life.

Second, the burden of hope is the responsibility that attends the bearer of the seed. The one who bears the seed is not just a container, but a sower! Seed can be borne in a bucket and stowed in a sack. Bearing the seed is to take up the responsibility that lies upon the sower to prepare the soil and to nurture the growth of the seed through to harvest. The burden of hope bears the responsibility for taking up life again when there has been foolishness and failure. This responsibility is not only to sow the seed, but also to carry the hope of others whose livelihood depends upon the harvest!

To be a sower one must not only accept the yoke of life and enter into partnership with the creative power of God, but also engender the trust of others in the process. In the pocket of the sower, are not only the seeds of a future crop, but also the hopes of all who depend upon the harvest which is promised.

The gift of faith is not the burden. Rather, faith is the empowerment of God to bear the burden of hope and to sow and tend the seed. This seed is an investment of something precious to us in utter dependence upon the promise of a harvest through a power over which we have no control. Our hope, finally, is in God, not in the harvest of our own ambition. When we open the window of hope to the spiritual power of God's love, we find healing for our hurts and hope for our hearts.

The power of the seed is its capacity to draw what it needs from the limitless resources around it, provided that it is sown! This is why the metaphor of sowing is such an apt one for the discovery of hope through faith. Though our faith be as small as a mustard seed, Jesus reminded us, it can move mountains (Matthew 17:20). This is not because of the power which resides in the seed, for it is helpless until it is sown. The power comes from the source upon which faith draws. When our hope is in God, we draw upon his limitless love as the source of our faith.

When we feel overburdened, we need to ask ourselves why we are carrying the burden of life at all, not which burdens are the right ones? The burdens which we carry by the power of faith and hope are the burdens of the sower who has no control over the harvest. Spiritual fitness is not the capability to carry heavy burdens, but it is the gift of faith and the vision of hope by which every burden becomes a seed sown into the soil which we cultivate and water, but for which God alone can bring the harvest.

For this to happen, we must understand that when the soul is disconnected from its own source of life in the world, it will not only be undernourished and overburdened but also rendered powerless.

A well known speaker and author recently described the collapse of his frantic but highly successful life and career as a downward spiral and crash resulting from the 'disconnect' between the inner life of his soul and the outer construct of the self.[101] The disconnect between his soul and his public life produced emotional pain and spiritual bankruptcy. I would say that he was starving his soul while feeding his ego. When we become disconnected at the core of the self, we often redouble our efforts to gain control only to end on the slippery slope of spiritual suicide.

The spirituality of the New Age movement tends to disconnect the 'higher self' from the 'lower self' in an attempt to escape the pull of gravity which anchors the soul to an earthbound and temporal existence. True spirituality comes as a gift of soul which brings wisdom and grace into life.

Spiritual wisdom is not to disconnect from the reality of life when it sometimes brings pain and causes stress. Rather, it is to connect the soul to the source of life through the infusion of grace by resting in the sufficiency of the Word of God inspired by the efficacy of the Spirit of God.

Spiritual wisdom is not to escape the heavy burdens of life in favor of those that are weightless but may also be contentless. Rather, it is to know which burdens are worth bearing and which are not.

Spiritual wisdom is not gained by starving the soul through denial of our human needs. Rather it is discovered in being nourished by the 'bread of life' which comes down from heaven. "I am the living bread that came down from heaven," said Jesus. "Whoever eats of this bread will live forever" (John 6:51). Live forever? Is that a promise? What if it is true!

TEN

The Resurrection of the Soul: A Vision of Life Beyond Death

I am a believer in the afterlife... If there is no afterlife, much of what I have been saying is rot. (M. Scott Peck)[102]

    Our journey with New Age spirituality has come to an end. I want to speak of death and resurrection of both soul and body, but I find no interest in the subject. I wish to explore the promise of heaven and the continuation of my individual life and soul beyond the grave, but those who teach New Age spirituality apparently have no desire or need for personal identity in a life to come. The fact that every teacher of New Age spirituality and every person who subscribes to the healing power of New Age thought will sooner or later no longer exist on this earth does not seem to dampen their enthusiasm or shatter their optimism.

    The word 'death' is seldom found in their vocabulary, nor is there any vision of personal, self-conscious, life beyond death. The only mention of death in Gary Zukav's book is in the case of a child that dies early in life. In this case, says Zukav, "we do not know what agreement was made between the child's soul and the soul of its parents, or what healing was served by that experience. Although we are sympathetic to the anguish of the parents, we cannot judge this event."[103] Really? It is true that we do not always understand why death occurs, but we surely must not seek to ease the pain of death by viewing it as a friend, when in reality it is an enemy of the soul.

Is there no room in New Age spirituality for the soul's protest against the senseless extinguishing of life? "Do not go gently into that good night; Rage, rage against the dying of the light!"[104] Are there no words of comfort to be found such as offered by Jesus? "Do not let your hearts be troubled. Believe in God, believe also in me. In my Father's house there are many dwelling places. If it were not so, would I have told you that I go to prepare a place for you? And if I go and prepare a place for you, I will come again and will take you to myself, so that where I am, there you may be also" (John 14:1-3).

In New Age spirituality there are no images of hell—for which some might well give thanks. But there is also no language for heaven—which leaves the soul with a spiritual void for which there are no words. The haunting words of Thomas Wolfe urge us to continue where many turn back: "Remembering speechlessly we seek the great forgotten language, the lost lane-end into heaven, a stone, a leaf, an unfound door. Where? When?"[105]

We have appreciation for the emphasis of any spiritual focus on the healing and health of the inner self. Traditional forms of Christian teaching have often left a void which more contemporary forms of spirituality rush to fill. I have sought to demonstrate that a biblical concept of the spiritual nature of the human soul is wholistic and expansive. At points, there may not have appeared to be much difference between a spirituality generated out of the soul's own capacity and that which results from the gracious gift and renewing presence of the Holy Spirit. I acknowledge that. There is ambiguity which may only be resolved as we press forward.

I question New Age spirituality and its concept of

the soul with regard to its adequacy, not its efficiency. For example, Gary Zukav's concept of the soul is a marvel of efficiency. It even has a certain elegance to it. The soul, as he depicts it, dances to the classical strains of Mozart, while the personality jitterbugs to the frenzied, pulsing beat of emotions and moods. The soul is the landscaper of the libidinous life, soothing the rough edges of emotional pain. In his view, the soul is a cathedral offering sacred repose for the convulsive and compulsive personality. New Age spirituality is the artificial turf spread over the raw clay of creaturely existence, much like the mortician uses fake green grass to cover the fresh earth at the gravesite. It is all very efficient, but is it adequate?

I do not find it so. The soul as viewed in New age thought is immortal soul, but without a name and face. It survives the death of the body, but not the extinguishing of personality. In new age thought, the ultimate home of the soul is not a place of blessed reunion with other souls but a pool of unification with something called eternal soul. As someone once said of a certain city, "there is no *there* there!"

Scott Peck wrote, "when I was still on the lecture circuit, the question I was asked most frequently was not whether I believed in an afterlife but whether I believed in reincarnation." His response was, "Whether we had a previous existence before our conception and birth seems to me an issue of relatively little consequence. On the other hand, the question of whether there is life after death—an afterlife—strikes me as absolutely crucial."[106]

Peck's concern is not for a theological map of the afterlife, but for the conviction of the soul that such a life exists as the substance of faith which gives meaning to this life and hope in the face of death. "It is human to be frightened of going into the unknown," he writes, "and personally I am terrified of dying. I don't even have a map. 'My God, my God, no not forsake me,' I'll be praying. At the same time I'll be believing. There's something more ahead of us, but God knows what it is."[107]

I like his candor. I do not believe as he does that the soul has natural immortality, but I believe that both soul and body will be given the gift of immortality through resurrection. There is more ahead of us!

Jesus was equally candid about his own fear in the face of dying, but more specific about the reality of life beyond death. "Now is my soul troubled," he cried out as he saw certain death looming on the horizon of his life (John 12:27). Yet, with utmost confidence he confided to his disciples, "I am going to the Father... If you loved me, you would rejoice that I am going to the Father, because the Father is greater than I... And now I am no longer in the world, but they are in the world, and I am coming to you" (John 14:12, 28; 17:11).

The 'place' to which Jesus was going was not only a place where he could be rejoined with the Father, but also a place where others could be reunited with him and with each other beyond death. "I will not leave you orphaned," Jesus promised..... And if I go and prepare a place for you, I will come again and will take you to myself, so that where I am, there you may be also" (John 14:18, 2-3).

The most explicit references to resurrection and life after death in the New Testament are found in the writings of the apostle Paul. He accounts for his own conversion to faith in Jesus as the Messiah as resulting from a personal encounter with the risen Christ who appeared to him on the road to Damascus. This was not described as a 'near death' experience, but as an event that took place in public where others saw and heard phenomena related to the encounter (Acts 9; 22:6-21; 26:12-18).[108]

The core of Paul's apostolic preaching and teaching rested on the historical and factual event of the resurrection of Jesus after three days in the tomb. This included the promise that those who believed in Jesus would also be resurrected to experience life with God and with

The Resurrection of the Soul

others following death.

"For I handed on to you as of first importance what I in turn had received: that Christ died for our sins in accordance with the scriptures, and that he was buried, and that he was raised on the third day in accordance with the scriptures, and that he appeared to Cephas, then to the twelve. Then he appeared to more than five hundred brothers and sisters at one time, most of whom are still alive, though some have died. Then he appeared to James, then to all the apostles. Last of all, as to one untimely born, he appeared also to me. For I am the least of the apostles, unfit to be called an apostle, because I persecuted the church of God" (1 Corinthians 15:3-9).

The reality of the resurrection of Jesus was so crucial to Paul that he considered the death of Jesus on the cross to have no significance and merit apart from the resurrection. "If Christ has not been raised, your faith is futile and you are still in your sins. Then those also who have died in Christ have perished. If for this life only we have hoped in Christ, we are of all people most to be pitied" (1 Corinthians 15:17-19). When questioned as to the nature of the resurrection body Paul could only use an analogy drawn from nature. As the seed is sown in the ground, it emerges in a totally new form, yet there is continuity between the two forms. In the same way, he argues, our physical body is "sown in dishonor and weakness," but raised in glory and in power. "It is sown a physical body, it is raised a spiritual body. If there is a physical body, there is also a spiritual body" (1 Corinthians 15:44). Without explaining how this takes place, Paul simply states it as fact based upon the resurrection of Jesus.

The argument for life after death is not based on the concept of an immortal soul, but upon the resurrection of the body. If Paul had believed that it was the soul that survived death as the bearer of personal identity, then resurrection of the body would not have been necessary, though naturally, there would be some interest in it. On the contrary, Paul viewed the resurrection of the body as essential to the continued existence of persons following death.

In Paul's discussion of life after death there is no reference to a 'spiritual' soul which would replace the creaturely soul in somewhat the same way as the 'spiritual' body replaces the 'physical' body. This is clear because, for Paul, it is not the power of a natural, immortal soul that insures life after death, but the nature of Jesus Christ.

Paul compares Adam as representative of all who are 'from the dust' and subject to mortality with Jesus Christ who bears Adam's humanity but is 'from heaven.' "The first man was from the earth, a man of dust; the second man is from heaven. As was the man of dust, so are those who are of the dust; and as is the man of heaven, so are those who are of heaven. Just as we have borne the image of the man of dust, we will also bear the image of the man of heaven" (1 Corinthians 15:47-49). What provides assurance of continuity of the self through death and resurrection is not an immortal soul but the granting of immortality to the mortal human person as a body/soul unity, as having already taken place on our behalf through the resurrection of Christ.

The soul is the mortal life of the body and the new life in a 'spiritual' body given by God after death which corresponds to the 'physical' body, is now an immortal life. The soul which was the mortal life of physical body now becomes the immortal life of the spiritual body. The source of this transformation is said by Paul to be in the power of resurrection rather than in a natural, immortal soul.

New Testament scholar, Murray Harris argues persuasively that the issue of "what part of the person survives death" is irrelevant, as there is no suggestion in Paul's thought that a 'soul' survives death as a disembodied substance awaiting a 'spiritual body.' "In Pauline thought it is not the soul but 'this mortal body' (*to thnenton*

The Resurrection of the Soul

touto) that is destined to put on immortality, to become immortal through a somatic resurrection (1 Cor. 15:53-54); it is not by birth, but by grace, and through resurrection, that immortality is gained."[109]

There have always been those throughout the ages who wish to view the soul as immortal. Through all of history there has always been a form of 'New Age' religious thought with a concept of a pre-existing immortal soul which takes up temporary residence in an earthly personality and body. This type of humanistic philosophy answers the problem of death by asserting that death only affects the body not the soul. However, in New Age thought, the personality as well as the body expires leaving the soul to return to an undifferentiated ocean of eternal soul. There is no 'after life' for the personality.

I can also understand the conviction of Scott Peck who views the denial of an immortal soul on the part of a reductionist, secular culture as a tragic loss of meaning and hope for an afterlife on the part of persons who are dying. The soul, for Peck, has no prior existence. It is apparently created for each person by God as an immortal soul which does not die. This does not solve the problem of death, but it makes dying a transition into a new state of being. The concern for an immortal soul is understandable in the face of the inevitability of death for every person. Thinking of the soul as an immortal substance dwelling in mortal body is one way of answering the question as to what happens at the point of death.

It is not necessary, however, to think of the nature of the soul as immortal in order to believe in life after death. The issue is not the nature of the soul, but the possibility of life after death. Immortality belongs to God alone, as the Bible clearly teaches. "It is he alone who has immortality and dwells in unapproachable light, whom no one has ever seen or can see; to him be honor and eternal dominion. Amen" (1 Timothy 6:16). If immortality is given to persons after death by the power of

God, rather than a natural attribute of the soul, death has been overcome by life, and there is an afterlife for real persons, not merely for impersonal 'soul.'

The Bible does not support the concept of the human soul as an immortal substance residing in a mortal body. What the Bible does insist, however, is that God alone possesses immortality and God can and will take what is mortal (from the dust) and give it the gift of immortality through death and resurrection. Why should there be a problem with accepting the biblical concept of a mortal body and soul if both are granted immortality and life after death through resurrection? Is not this more satisfying than a theory of reincarnation which asserts that each person had a prior existence which is unknown and not remembered and a future incarnation which is experienced by a different self? And rather than having to argue for the existence of an invisible, intangible, metaphysical substance called immortal soul, is it not more meaningful (and humble!) to allow God the power to preserve both body and soul through death and resurrection as the basis for our belief in an afterlife?

In acknowledging the power of God to create a human soul 'out of nothing' and endowing it with an immortal nature, one must also expect the power of God to transform mortal human souls and bodies through death into an immortal state. The claim to have a divine, immortal soul is a claim to be 'like God,' which was the original temptation to humans in the biblical account of the fall. Some, like Gary Zukav does not hesitate to make this claim: "You have always been because what it is that you are is God."[110]

Even more traditional theologians who insist that the soul is immortal come close to asserting that the soul has replaced God as the source of immortality. The belief that the soul is immortal could enable one to die with some confidence in a future life of the soul without a sustaining belief in God. After all, it may not be so much that our contemporary secular culture has 'denied the soul,' as Scott Peck suggests, but that it has 'denied God.'

What causes the apostle Paul apprehension in the face of death is not death itself, but being 'unclothed,' that is, to be without a body. "For while we are still in this tent, we groan under our burden, because we wish not to be unclothed but to be further clothed, so that what is mortal may be swallowed up by life" (2 Corinthians 5:4). Did Paul consider the possibility of living as a disembodied soul after his death, awaiting resurrection? If so, he seems to dismiss the idea immediately. Rather, he has confidence in an afterlife with direct experience of Christ the Lord as preferable to living with the sufferings of this present world. "So we are always confident; even though we know that while we are at home in the body we are away from the Lord— for we walk by faith, not by sight. Yes, we do have confidence, and we would rather be away from the body and at home with the Lord" (2 Corinthians 5:6-8).

This, of course, opens up the question which has plagued many theologians—if the soul is immortal and survives death, what is the state of the soul between the point of death and resurrection of the body? Some argue for the existence of a self-conscious, disembodied soul between death and resurrection, as a way of assuring personal identity and continuity between death and resurrection.[111] This seems to be more of a philosophical problem, however, than a theological one. Except for the apostle Paul's rather indirect mention of being 'unclothed,' the Bible does not encourage us to think in this way.

The New Testament is not concerned for a 'state' which exists between death and resurrection, but for a 'relation' which exists between the person and Christ through death. Theologian Helmut Thielicke concludes, "The removal of a sense of time means for those who are awakened that the long night of death is reduced to a mathematical point, and they are thus summoned out of a complete life."[112] In support of this, Thomas Torrance says, "Looked at from the perspective of the new creation there is no gap between the death of the believer and the *parousis*a of Christ, but looked at from the perspective of time that decays and crumbles away, there is a lapse of time between them."[113]

Children ask questions about death out of curiosity. Their innocence permits them this luxury. They have not yet learned that the most holy and the most intimate do not yield their secrets to the curious. Whether the terror of death is the approach of the holy we are not sure. But we do know by now that death is far too intimate for us to ply questions merely out of curiosity.

On a lazy summer Sunday afternoon, without apparent premeditation, my parents would suddenly announce a trip to the local rural cemetery for the purpose of tending some family grave sites. Of course we children were included. It was not a long trip, for the cemetery adjoined the farm on which we lived on the flat prairie-land of middle America. The simple rituals of pulling some weeds, clipping some grass and digging up the soil around a straggling, flowering plant were quickly accomplished, and served only as a pretext for the visit, as it usually turned out.

Trailing behind, as my parents wandered from grave site to grave site, I heard the litany of their commentary on the dead. "Here's where the Torstensons are buried. Wasn't she a Carlson girl who came over with her parents from the old country, and didn't they homestead the quarter section next to the old Anderson farm where I was born?" my father would ask.

And so it went. These were not questions, but statements: statements about a community in which the boundary between the living and the dead lost its sharp edge of terror. This was a mystery which was part of the fabric of life. What this small boy experienced was the easy familiarity with which this uncanny boundary

The Resurrection of the Soul

was traversed. But even more, what was experienced was the wordless testimony that this excursion was an event in which their faith was enacted. Implicit in this patriarchal pageantry was a statement about what they believed, and death was not alien to this belief system.

What did my father think about when he tended the gravesites and contemplated the plot where he himself would one day be buried? Did he have anxiety? Did he fear that death would annihilate all of the meaning of his life to that point? Did he have the feeling that he was sinking into an oblivion which would be a place of peace and rest from self-conscious worry and fretful toil? Or did he have in his mind a hope for continuing self conscious life beyond the grave, and if so, how did he envision this? He never said. But he lived as though it were true and died with the promise of Jesus nourishing his soul.

The final stop, before getting into the car, was always a quiet moment spent tidying a green plot with no graves yet dug, marked only with the single headstone - ANDERSON. This plot has now been filled, of course. And not too far away there is another plot which has been purchased which not only signals my own anticipation of joining this 'processional', but which is also a statement about what I believe, about life and about death. I am not, because of distance, granted the privilege of being the 'caretaker' of my own place of burial, nor have my children ever visited the site.

What will they believe about death? And what are the resources out of which they will create that belief? Obviously they are not the same as mine. Yet, from childhood on, we search for an answer to the phenomenon of death and, one way or another, come to think about our own death and reach out for assurance that our life, in some form, will continue more radiantly and gloriously than we dare to dream. This is the conviction that shapes the life of the soul and inspired Sister Madeleva to sing:

And this clay will pass from me, and life,
    aye, and death, like a vapor;
I shall rise at His word, light as light,
    quick as thought, swift as wing,
For though dust, soul of mine,
    even dust in the hands of its Shaper
Is a glorified thing.[114]

Bibliography of Works Cited

Anderson, Ray S. *The Gospel According to Judas: Is There a Limit to God's Forgiveness?* Colorado Springs: NavPress, 1991, 1994

Anderson, Ray S. *On Being Human—Essays in Theological Anthropology.* Grand Rapids: Eerdmans Publishing Company, 1982.

Anderson, Ray S. "On Being Human: The Spiritual Saga of a Creaturely Soul," in *Whatever Happened to the Soul? Scientific and Theological Portraits of Human Nature.* Warren S. Brown, Nancey Murphy and H. Newton Malony, editors. Minneapolis: Fortress Press, 1998, pp. 175-194.

Anderson, Ray S. *Self Care: A Theology of Personal Empowerment and Spiritual Healing.* Wheaton: Victor Books and Grand Rapids: Baker Books, 1995

Anderson, Ray S. *Theology, Death and Dying.* Oxford: Basil Blackwell, 1986

Ashbrook, James B. "Different Voices, Different Genes: 'Male and Female Created God *Them*'," in *Christian Perspectives on Sexuality and Gender*, Adrian Thatcher and Elizabeth Stuart, eds. Grand Rapids: Eerdmans, 1996

Ashley, Benedict M O. P. *Theologies of the Body: Humanist and Christian.* Braintree, MA: The Pope John Center, 1985

Aquinas, Thomas. *Selected Philosophical Writings*, selected and translated by T. McDermot. Oxford: Oxford University Press, 1993

Becker, Ernest. *The Denial of Death.* New York: The Macmillan Company, The Free Press, 1975

Bellah, Robert, et al. *Habits of the Heart—Individualism and Commitment in American Life.* Berkeley: University of California Press, 1985

Benson, Herbert, M. D. *Beyond the Relaxation Response.* New York: Times Books, 1984.

Blake. William. *Oxford Poetry Library.* Oxford: Oxford University Press, 1994
Bonhoeffer, Dietrich. *Sanctorum Communio* (Communion of Saints). Minneapolis: Fortress Press, 1998 edition
Boyd, Jeffrey H. "The Soul as Seen Through Evangelical Eyes, Part II: Mental Health Professionals and the 'Soul'," in *Journal of Psychology and Theology,* 1995, Vol. 23, #3, pp.161-170
Bradshaw, John. *Bradshaw On: Healing the Shame that Binds You.* Deerfield Beach, FL: Health Communications, 1988
Brown, Warren S. , Murphy, Nancey, and H. Newton Malony editors. *Whatever Happened to the Soul? Scientific and Theological Portraits of Human Nature.* Minneapolis: Fortress Press, 1998
Browning, Elizabeth Barrett. *Sonnets from the Portuguese and Other Love Poems.* Garden City, NY: Hanover House, 1954
Brunner, Emil. *Man in Revolt.* London: Lutterworth Press, 1939; reprint, Philadelphia: Westminster Press, 1979
Buber, Martin. *I and Thou,* tr. by Walter Kaufman. Edinburgh: T. & T. Clark, 1979
Capps, Donald. "The Soul as the 'Coreness' of the Self," *The Treasure of Earthen Vessels—Explorations into Theological Anthropology,* eds. Brian H. Childs and David W. Waanders. Louisville: WestminsterJohn Knox Press, 1994
Carse, James B. *Death and Existence.* New York: John Wiley, 1980
Cerfaaux. L. *The Christian in the Theology of St. Paul.* London: Chapman, 1967
Chandler. Russell. *Understanding the New Age.* Grand Rapids: Zondervan: (1988) 1991 (revised, updated).
Chopra, Deepak. *Ageless Body, Timeless Mind—The Quantum Alternative to growing Old.* New York: Crown Trade Paperbaks, 1984
Chopra, Deepak. *Everyday Immortality: A Concise Course in Spiritual Transformation.* New York: Harmony Books, 1999
Chopra, Deepak, *The Path to Love: Renewing the Power of Spirit in Your Life.* New York: Harmony Books, 1997
Chopra, Deepak. *Healing the Heart: A Spiritual Approach to Reversing Coronary Artery Disease.* New York: Harmony Books, 1998
Collins, Kenneth. *Soul Care: Deliverance and Renewal Through the Christian Life.* Wheaton: Victor Books, 1995

Cooper, John W. *Body, Soul, & Life Everlasting—Biblical Anthropology and the Monism-Dualism Debate*. Grand Rapids: Eerdmans Publishing Company, 1989

Cox, Harvey. *Religion in the Secular City: Toward a Postmodern Theology*. New York: Simon and Schuster, 1984.

Cox, Harvey. *Fire From Heaven: The Rise of Pentecostal Spirituality and the Reshaping of Religion in the Twenty-First Century*. Reading, Mass.: Addison-Wesley Pubishers,1995

Crosby, Robert. *Living Life From the Soul: How a Man Unleashes God's Power from the Inside Out*. Minneapolis: Bethany House Publishers, 1997

Demarest, Bruce, *Satisfy Your Soul: Restoring the Heart of Christian Spirituality*. Colorado Springs: NavPress, 1999

Dickinson, Emily. *The Complete Poetry of Emily Dickinson*. Boston: Little Brown and Company, 1989

Donne, John. *The Poems of John Donne*, H. J. C. Grierson, editor. London: Oxford University Press, 1964.

Dossey, Larry. *Healing Words: The Power of Prayer and the Practice of Medicine*. San Francisco: HarperSanFrancisco, 1993.

Drane, John. *What is the New Age Saying to the Church?*, London: Marshal Pickering, an imprint of HarperCollinsPublishers, 1991.

Dueck, Alvin. *Between Jerusalem and Athens: Ethical Perspectives on Culture, Religion, and Psycotherapy*. Grand Rapids: Baker Books, 1995.

Eichrodt, W. *Theology of the Old Testament*, Vol. 2, Philadelphia: Westminster Press, 1975

Ellison, Craig. *Your Better Self: Christianity, Psychology, and Self-Esteem*. New York: Harper and Row, 1983

Fox, Matthew. *Original Blessing: A Primer in Creation Spirituality Presented in Four Paths, Twenty-six Themes, and Two Questions*. Sante Fe, NM: Bear & Co., 1983.

Fox, Matthew. *The Coming of the Cosmic Christ: The Healing of Mother Earth and the Birth of a Global Renaissance*. San Francisco: Harper and Row, 1988.

Fry, Christopher. *The Boy With a Cart*. New York: Oxford University Press, 1959

Fry, Christopher. *Sleep of Prisoners.* London: Oxford University Press, 1951

Gallop, George. "Buddhist Practices Make Inroads in the US," *The Christian Science Monitor.* November 3, 1997

Gerkin, Charles. *The Living Human Document—Re-Visioning Pastoral Counseling in a Hermeneutical Mode.* Nashville: Abingdon, 1984

Hanegraaff. Wouter J. *New Age Religion and Western Culture: Esotericism in the Mirror of Secular Thought.* Leiden; New York: E.J. Brill, 1996

Harris, Murray J. *From the Grave to Glory: Resurrection in the New Testament.* Grand Rapids: Zondervan, 1990

Harris. Murray J. *Raised Immortal—Resurrection and Immortality in the New.* Grand Rapids: Eerdmans Publishing Company, 1983.

Hart, Archibald. *Unlocking the Mystery of your Emotions* . Dallas: Word Publishing, 1979, 1989

Heelas, Paul.*The New Age Movement: The Celebration of the Self and the Sacralization of Modernity.* Oxford ; Cambridge, Mass., Blackwell, 1996

Hill, Edmund. *Being Human: A Biblical Perspective.* London: Geoffrey Chapman, 1984

Hirsch, R. D. "Two Sides of the Soul," *Journal of Reformed Judaism*, Vol. xxxvi, No. 2, (Spring, 1989), pp. 17-26.

Kaplan, Marty. "Ambushed by Spirituality," *Time* Magazine, June 24, 1996, Volume 147, No. 26,

Karen, Robert. "Shame," *The Atlantic Monthly*, Volume 269, No. 2, February, 1992

Koester, Helmut. *Introduction to the New Testament*, Vol. I. New York: Walter de Gruyter, 1995, 2nd edition.

Kushner, Lawrence. *Honey From the Rock.* Woodstock, Vermont: Jewish Lights Press, 1994

Levang, Curtis. *The Adam and Eve Complex—Freedom from the Shame that Can Separate you from God, Others, and Yourself* (Minneapolis: SelfCare Books, 1992),

McDonald, Gordon. *The Life God Blesses.* Nashville: Thomas Nelson Publishers, 1994

MacLaine, Shirley. *Out on a Limb.* New York: Bantam Books, 1984

MacLaine, Shirley. *Dancing in the Light.* Toronto: Bantam Books, 1985

Macmurray, John. *Persons in Relation.* London: Faber and Faber, 1961

McRoberts. Kerry D. *New Age or Old Lie?* Peabody, Mass.: Hendrickson Publishers, 1989

McWaters, Barry. *Conscious Evolution.* Los Angeles: New Age Press, 1981.

Madeleva, Sister. *The Four Last things—Collected Poems.* New York: The Macmillan Company, 1959

Mangalwadi, Vishal. *When the New Age Gets Old: Looking for a Greater Spirituality.* Downers Grove: InterVarsity Press, 1992

Meissner, W. W. *Life and Faith: Psychological Perspectives on Religious Experience.* Washington, D.C.: Georgetown University Press, 1987

Melton, J. Gordon, Jerome Clark and Aidan A. Kelly. *New Age Encyclopedia: A Guide to the Beliefs, Concepts, Terms, People, and Organizations that Make up the New Global Movement Toward Spiritual Development, Health and Healing, Higher Consciousness, and Related Subjects.* Detroit, Mich.: Gale Research, 1990.

Menninger, Karl A. *Whatever Became of Sin?* New York : Hawthorn Books, 1973

Millay, Edna St. Vincent. "Wine from these Grapes," sonnet 10, in *Collected Poems*, ed. Norman Millay. New York: Harper and Row, 1956

Miller, Elliot. *A Crash Course on the New Age Movement: Describing and Evaluating a Growing Social Force.* Grand Rapids: Baker Book House, 1989

Miller, J. Keith. *Taste of New Wine.* Waco, TX. Word Books, 1966

Miller, J. Keith. *The Secret Life of the Soul.* Nashville: Broadman and Holman, Publishers, 1997

Monroe, Robert. *Journeys Out of the Body.* Garden City, NY: Anchor Press, 1973

Moore, Thomas. *Care of the Soul: A Guide for Cultivating Depth and Sacredness in Everyday Life.* New York: Harper Collins, 1992

Mowrer, O. Hobart. *The Crisis of Psychiatry and Religion.* Princeton, NJ: Van Nostrand, 1961.

O'Neil, Eugene. "The Great God Brown," *The Plays of Eugene O'Neil.* New York: Modern Library. 1982

Peck, S. Scott. *Denial of the Soul: Spiritual and Medical Perspectives on Euthanasia and Mortality.* New York: Harmony Books, 1997

Peters, Ted. *The Cosmic Self: A Penetrating Look at Today's New Age Movements.* San Francisco: HarperSanFrancisco, 1991.

Prophet, Elizabeth Clare. *The Lost Years of Jesus.* Livingston, MT: Summit University Press, 1987

Rhodes, Ron *The New Age Movement.* Grand Rapids: Zondervan, 1995

Roark, Dallas M. *The Christian Faith.* Nashville, Broadman Press, 1969

Sister Madeleva, *The Four Last Things—Collected Poems.* New York: The Macmillan Company, 1959

Smedes, Lewis B. *Shame and Grace—Healing the Shame We Don't Deserve.* San Francisco: Harper and Row, 1993

Talbot, Michael. *Mysticism and the New Physics.* New York: Bantam Books, 1981

Thielicke, Helmut. *Living with Death.* Grand Rapids: Eerdmans, 1983

Thomas, Dylan. *The Poems of Dylan Thomas.* New York: New Directions Publications, 1971

Thompson, Francis, "The Kingdom of Heaven," *The Selected Poems of Francis Thompson.* London: Burns and Oates, 1907

Torrance, Thomas F. *Space, Time and Resurrection.* Grand Rapids: Eerdmans, 1976

Trible, Phyllis. *God and the Rhetoric of Sexuality.* Philadelphia: Fortress Press, 1978

Vander Goot, Mary. *Healthy Emotions: Helping Children Grow.* Grand Rapids: Baker Books House, 1987

Webster, Douglas D. *Soulcraft: How God Shapes us Through Relationships.* Downers Grove: InterVarsity Press, 1999

Wells, Claudia. "Faith and Healing," *Time* Magazine, June 24, 1996 Volume 147, No. 26.

Wolfe, Thomas. *Look Homeward Angel!* New York: Charles Scribner's Sons, 1930

Zukav, Gary. *The Seat of the Soul.* New York: Simon and Schuster,

1989
Zukav, Gary. *Thoughts from the Seat of the Soul: Meditations for Souls in Process.* New York: Simon & Schuster, 1994
Zukav, Gary. *The Dancing Wu-Li Masters: An Overview of the New Physics.* New York: William Morrow and Co., 1979.

Endnotes

1. "Ambushed by Spirituality," in *Time Magazine*, June 24, 1996, Volume 147, No. 26,

2. Christopher Fry, *Sleep of Prisoners* (London: Oxford University Pess, 1951), p. 49.

3. *Care of the Soul: A Guide for Cultivating Depth and Sacredness in Everyday Life* (New York: Harper Collins, 1992, p. xi.

4. Thomas Moore, *Care of the Soul: A Guide for Cultivating Depth and Sacredness in Everyday Life* (New York: Harper Collins, 1992, p. xi.

5. S. Scott Peck, *Denial of the Soul: Spiritual and Medical Perspectives on Euthanasia and Mortality* (New York: Harmony Books, 1997), p. 129.

6. Ernest Becker, *The Denial of Death* (New York: The Macmillan Company, The Free Press, 1975).

7. Zukav, Gary. *The Seat of the Soul* (New York : Simon and Schuster, 1989), pp. 31ff.

8. *The Secret Life of the Soul*, J. Keith Miller (Nashville: Broadman and Holman, Publishers, 1997), p. 5.

9. "Ambushed by Spirituality," in *Time* Magazine, June 24, 1996, Volume 147, No. 26,

10. Michael Talbot. *Mysticism and the New Physics* (New York: Bantam Books, 1981), pp. 54, 152.

11. *Religion in the Secular City: Toward a Postmodern Theology* (New York : Simon and Schuster, 1984). *Fire From Heaven: The Rise of Pentecostal Spirituality and the Reshaping of Religion in the Twenty-First Century* (Reading, Mass.: Addison-Wesley Pub.,1995).

12. John Drane. *What is the New Age Saying to the Church* (London: Marshal Pickering, an imprint of HarperCollinsPublishers), 1991, p. 45.

13. Russell Chandler, *Understanding the New Age* (Grand Rapids: Zondervan Publishing House, 1993, revised and updated edition), p. 43.

14. *New Age Encyclopedia: A Guide to the Beliefs, Concepts, Terms, People, and Organizations that Make up the New Global Movement*

Toward Spiritual Development, Health and Healing, Higher Consciousness, and Related Subjects. J. Gordon Melton, Jerome Clark and Aidan A. Kelly. 1st ed (Detroit, Mich.: Gale Research, 1990). See also: Russell Chandler. *Understanding the New Age* (Dallas: Word Publishing, 1988). Paul Heelas. *The New Age Movement: The Celebration of the Self and the Sacralization of Modernity* (Oxford ; Cambridge, Mass., Blackwell, 1996). Wouter J. Hanegraaff. *New Age Religion and Western Culture: Esotericism in the Mirror of Secular Thought* (Leiden ; New York: E.J. Brill,). Kerry D. McRoberts. *New Age or Old Lie?* (Peabody, Mass.: Hendrickson Publishers, 1989). Ron Rhodes, *The New Age Movement* (Grand Rapids: Zondervan, 1995).

15. Deepak Chopra. *Ageless Body, Timeless Mind—The Quantum Alternative to Growing Old.* (New York: Crown Trade Paperbacks,1994). See also, *Everyday Immortality : A Concise Course in Spiritual Transformation* (New York: Harmony Books, 1999); *The Path to Love: Renewing the Power of Spirit in Your Life* (New: Harmony Books,1997); *Healing the Heart: A Spiritual Approach to Reversing Coronary Artery Disease* (New York: Harmony Books, 1998).

16. See: Herbert Benson, M. D. *Beyond the Relaxation Response* (New York: Times Books, 1984);

17. Cited by Claudia Wells, "Faith and Healing," *Time* Magazine, June 24, 1996 Volume 147, No. 26.

18. Larry Dossey, *Healing Words : The Power of Prayer and the Practice of Medicine* (San Francisco: HarperSanFrancisco, 1993), p. 198.

19. Dossey, p. 60.

20. Barry McWaters, *Conscious Evolution* (Los Angeles: New Age Press, 1981), pp. 111-112.

21. Russell Chandler, *Understanding the New Age* (Grand Rapids: Zondervan Publishing House, 1993, revised and updated edition), p. 78.

22. Cited by John Drane, pp. 96-97.

23. Cited by John Drane, pp. 130131.

24. Robert Monroe, *Journeys Out of the Body* (Garden City, NY: Anchor Press, 1973), pp. 138-139. Cited by Drane, p. 131.

25. Elizabeth Clare Prophet, *The Lost Years of Jesus* (Livingston, MT: Summit University Press, 1987). Cited by Ted

Peters, *The Cosmic Self: A Penetrating Look at Today's New Age Movements* (San Francisco: HarperSanFrncisco, 1991), p. 88.

26. Zukav, Gary. *The Seat of the Soul* (New York : Simon and Schuster, 1989). See also his later book, *Thoughts from the Seat of the Soul : Meditations for Souls in Process* (New York: Simon & Schuster, 1994).

27. *The Seat of the Soul* (New York: Simon and Schuster, 1989)., pp. 31, 35-36).

28. *The Seat of the Soul*, p. 37,

29. *The Seat of the Soul*, pp. 197-98.

30. *The Seat of the Soul*, p. 186.

31. *The Seat of the Soul*, p. 89.

32. *The Seat of the Soul*, p. 241.

33. Elliot Miller. *A Crash Course on the New Age Movement: Describing and Evaluating a Growing Social Force* (Grand Rapids: Baker Book House, 1989), p. 44. See also, Wouter J. Hanegraff. *New Age Religions and Western Culture*, p. 106. As for the supposed scientific basis for Zukav's thought, see his earlier book, *The Dancing Wu-Li Masters: An Overview of the New Physics* (New York: William Morrow and Co. , 1979).

34. Wouter J. Hanegraaff. *New Age Religion and Western Culture : Esotericism in the Mirror of Secular Thought* (Leiden ; New York: E.J. Brill,, 1996). Hanegraaff asserts that new age religion, if one can even call it that, can only be seen in the mirror of western, secular thought. It is the esoteric aspect of the new age movement that differentiates it from the more empirical, rationalistic, and reductionistic views of reality in a secular view of life and the human condition. See also, Paul Heelas. *The New Age Movement: The Celebration of the Self and the Sacralization of Modernity* (Oxford: Cambridge, Mass., Blackwell, 1996).

35. *The Seat of the Soul*, p. 212

36. Matthew Fox, *Original Blessing: A Primer in Creation Spirituality Presented in Four Paths, Twenty-six Themes, and Two Questions* (Sante Fe, NM: Bear & Co., 1983), p. 82. See also his book, *The Coming of the Cosmic Christ: The Healing of Mother Earth and the Birth of a Global Renaissance* (San Francisco: Harper and Row, 1988).

37. *Dancing in the Light* (Toronto: Bantam Books, 1985), pp. 114-115

38. *The Denial of the Soul*, p. 132

39. Ernest Becker. *The Denial of Death*, p. 204.

40. The location of the soul within the body was a subject of ancient speculation, the liver being a prime candidate because, of all the bodily organs, it had the most remarkable capacity of regeneration. See, Donald Capps, "The Soul as the 'Coreness' of the Self," *The Treasure of Earthen Vessels--Explorations into Theological Anthropology*, eds. Brian H. Childs and David W. Waanders (Louisville: Westminster JohnKnox Press, 1994), pp. 91ff. Capps, in all seriousness, suggests that the soul might be located in the lower body of the digestive system and the spirit in the higher blood-vascular system, perhaps the heart! Ibid.

41. "The Spiritual Saga of a Creaturely Soul," Ray S. Anderson, in *Whatever Happened to the Soul? Scientific and Theological Portraits of Human Nature*. Warren S. Brown, Nancey Murphy and H. Newton Malony, editors (Minneapolis: Fortress Press, 1998).

42. Charles Gerkin describes the soul as the central core of the self: "To use the designation self is to emphasize the line of experienced continuity and interpretive capacity which emerges from the self's object relations. To use the term ego is to emphasize the coming together of a nexus of forces demanding mediation and compromise.... The term soul is here used as a theological term that points to the self's central core subject to the ego's conflicting forces and to the ultimate origins of the self in God. The soul is the gift of God bestowed upon the individual with the breath of life. It is thus the self, including its ego conflicts, as seen from an ultimate perspective--the perspective of the self as nurtured and sustained in the life of God." *The Living Human Document--Re-Visioning Pastoral Counseling in a Hermeneutical Mode* (Nashville: Abingdon, 1984), p. 98.

43. The Hebrew word nephesh, translated as 'soul,' is often coupled with other, more concrete words, especially with flesh (basar) and heart (lev, leva). Biblical Hebrew has no distinct word for 'body' as does the Greek (soma). Nephesh (soul) is often used in parallel with basar (flesh), never in contrast. The terms are not

used as a natural contrast such as 'body and soul,' but often virtually synonymous, being two ways of referring to the self in both its physical and non-physical existence. See, Ray S. Anderson, *On Being Human* (Grand Rapids: Eerdmans Publishing Company, 1982), pp. 209ff; Edmund Hill, *Being Human: A Biblical Perspective* (London: Geoffrey Chapman, 1984), p. 100

44. *Phaedo.* Cited by James B. Carse, *Death and Existence* (New York: John Wiley, 1980), pp. 12-13.

45. *The Denial of the Soul*, p. 132.

46. Ibid., p. 153.

47. I have discussed this further in, "On Being Human: The Spiritual Saga of a Creaturely Soul," in *Whatever Happened to the Soul? Scientific and Theological Portraits of Human Nature.* Warren S. Brown, Nancey Murphy and H. Newton Malony, editors (Minneapolis: Fortress Press, 1998), pp. 175-194.

48. W. Eichrodt reflects on Psalm 8:4 as follows: "Ultimately therefore it is a spiritual factor which determines the value Man sets upon himself, namely his consciousness of partnership with God, a privilege of which no other creation is considered worthy." *Theology of the Old Testament*, Vol. 2, pp. 120-1.

49. "For Man to be created in the likeness of God's image can only mean that on him, too, personhood is bestowed as the definitive characteristic of his nature. . . This quality of personhood shapes the totality of his psycho-physical existence; it is this which comprises the essentially human, and distinguishes him from all other creatures." W. Eichrodt, *Theology of the Old Testament*, Vol. 2, p. 126.

50. Spirit, wrote Dietrich Bonhoeffer, is necessarily created in community, and the general spirituality of persons is woven into the net of sociality. "It will appear that all Christian and moral content, as well as the entire spirituality of [persons], is possible and real only in sociality. Not only do the concepts of sin and of the church become more profound, but a way opens up to a Christian evaluation of community life. . . . Here we have to show that [a person's] entire so-called spirituality, which is presupposed by the Christian concept of person and has its unifying point in self-consciousness. . . is so constituted that it can only be seen as pos-

sible in sociality." *Sanctorum Communio* (Communion of Saints), 1927, first published, 1930 (Minneapolis: Fortress Press, 1998 edition); p. 73

51. Elizabeth Barrett Browning, *Sonnets from the Portuguese and Other Love Poems* (Garden City, NY: Hanover House, 1954), Sonnet #XXII, p. 36.

52. *Persons in Relation* (London: Faber and Faber, 1961), p. 159.

53. "Two wills encountering one another form a structure. A third person joining them sees not just one person connected to the other; rather, the will of the structure, as a third factor, resists the newcomer with a resistance not identical with the wills of the two individuals. Sometimes this is even more powerful than that of either individual--or than the sum of all the individuals, if this is at all conceivable. Precisely this structure is objective spirit." Dietrich Bonhoeffer, *Sanctorum Communio* (Communion of Saints) (Minneapolis: Fortress Press, 1998 edition), p. 98

54. Donne, John. *The Poems of John Donne*, H. J. C. Grierson, editor. London: Oxford University Press, 1964.

55. *Honey From the Rock*, Rabbi Lawrence Kushner, (Woodstock, Vermont: Jewish Lights Press, 1994).

56. Alvin Dueck, *Between Jerusalem and Athens: Ethical Perspectives on Culture, Religion, and Psycotherapy* (Grand Rapids: Baker Books, 1995), p. 202.

57. R. D. Hirsch "Two Sides of the Soul," *Journal of Reformed Judaism*, Vol. xxxvi, No. 2, (Spring, 1989), pp. 17-26.

58. "As presented in this first episode, with the definite article ha- preceding the common noun 'adam, this work of art is neither a particular person nor the typical person but rather the creature from the earth (ha-adama)--the earth creature. The very words that differentiate creature from soil indicate similarity. . . . More important, this creature is not identified sexually. Grammatical gender ('adam as a masculine word) is not sexual identification. . . In other words, the earth creature is not the male; it is not 'the first man.' . . His sexual identity depends upon her even as hers depends upon him. for both of them sexuality originates in the one flesh of humanity." Phyllis Trible, *God and the Rhetoric of Sexuality* (Philadelphia: Fortress Press, 1978), pp. 80, 99.

59. Based on recent scientific research on the brain, James B. Ashbrook, argues that sexual differentiation is 'hard wired' into the human brain. "As birth approaches, the masculinizing hormones, primarily testosterone, have so affected the development of the brain that a 'trained observer, holding a microscope slide [of the hypothalamus] up to the light, can tell the sex of the brain with the naked eye." "Different Voices, Different Genes: 'Male and Female Created God Them'," in *Christian Perspectives on Sexuality and Gender*, Adrian Thatcher and Elizabeth Stuart, eds. (Grand Rapids: Eerdmans, 1996), pp. 98-109; p. 102.

60. Psalms 32:1,2

61. Gary Zukav, *The Seat of the Soul* (New York: Simon and Schuster, 1989).

62. Zukav, *The Seat of the Soul*, p. 99.

63. "Grace is Uncontaminated Conscious Light. It is Divinity." Zukav, *The Seat of the Soul*, p. 241

64. Karl A Menninger, *Whatever Became of Sin?* (New York: Hawthorn Books, 1973)..

65. O. Hobart Mowrer, *The Crisis of Psychiatry and Religion* (Princeton, NJ: Van Nostrand, 1961), "So long as we subscribe to the view that neurosis is a bona fide 'illness,' without moral implications or dimensions, our position will of necessity continue to be an awkward one. . . We have tried the sickness horn of this dilemma and impaled ourselves upon it. Perhaps, despite our erstwhile protestations, we shall yet find sin more congenial." Pp. 50, 51.

66. Cited by Dallas M Roark, *The Christian Faith* (Nashville, Broadman Press,1969), pp. 151-2.

67. Ibid, pp. 155-6.

68. Russell Chandler, Religion writer for the *Los Angeles Times*, reports that "thirty-four million Americans are concerned with inner growth, including mysticism,. . . nearly half of American adults (42%) believe they have been in contact with someone who has died. . . .Roughly 30 million Americans—about one in four—now believe in reincarnation and 14% endorse the work of spirit mediums, or what New Agers often call 'trance channelers.'" *Understanding the New Age* (Grand Rapids: Zondervan, 1993), p. 20.

69. William Blake. *Oxford Poetry Library* (Oxford: Oxford University Press, 1994), pp. 263-4.

70. As quoted by Gordon McDonald, *The Life God Blesses* (Nashville: Thomas Nelson Publishers, 1994), p. 76.

71. Reported in *The Orange County Register*, October 14, 1999, p. 14.

72. *The Seat of the Soul*, p. 186.

73. Francis Thompson, "The Kingdom of Heaven," *The Selected Poems of Francis Thompson* (London: Burns and Oates, 1907), pp. 132-133.

74. *Man in Revolt* (Philadelphia: Westminster, 1939) p. 235.

75. Ernest Becker, *The Denial of Death* (New York: The Macmillan Company, The Free Press, 1975).

76. *The Secret Life of the Soul*, p. 65.

77. Christopher Fry: *Sleep of Prisoners* (London: Oxford University Press, 1951), p. 49.

78. Christopher Fry, *The Boy With a Cart* (New York: Oxford University Press, 1959), pp. 7-8.

79. Ibid., pp. 38, 39.

80. Emily Dickinson, *The Complete Poetry of Emily Dickinson* (Boston: Little Brown and Company, 1989).

81. Mary Vander Goot, *Healthy Emotions: Helping Children Grow* (Grand Rapids: Baker Books House, 1987), p. 43.

82. *The Boy with a Cart*, pp. 4. 8.

83. *The Seat of the Soul*, p. 241.

84. Eugene O'Neil, "The Great God Brown," *The Plays of Eugene O'Neil* (New York: Modern Library. 1982). 318.

85. *The Seat of the Soul*, pp. 29,30.

86. "Moral rules are based on a primitive level of development. They are derived from fear, a response to threats of abandonment, punishment, exposure, or the inner threat of guilt, shame, or isolation. Ethical rules, however, are based on ideals to be striven for.... There is a violence inherent in the moral sense. We violate children and arouse them to an inner rage when we keep them from the guidance and support they need to develop fully. Nonviolence means more than the preservation of another's physical inviolancy; it means the protection of his essence as a developing

person and personality." W. W. Meissner, *Life and Faith* (Washington, D.C.: Georgetown University Press, 1987), pp. 249; 252-2.

87. Robert Karen, "Shame," *The Atlantic Monthly*, Volume 269, No. 2, February, 1992, p. 41. John Bradshaw also speaks of a healthy and nourishing shame. *Bradshaw On: Healing the Shame that Binds You*, p. vii. "Healthy shame keeps us grounded. It is a yellow light warning us that we are essentially limited. Healthy shame is the basic metaphysical boundary for human beings. It is the emotional energy which signals us that we are not God--that we have made and will make mistakes, that we need help." (p. 4).

88. Lewis Smedes points to the spiritual nature of shame when he says: "Spiritual shame may come as a tremor after a close encounter with God, but unhealthy shame is a godless shame. Undeserved shame may come from religion, but it only gets in God's way. Religion without grace can tie shame around our souls like a choke chain and never offer relief. The pain we feel is not even a distant cousin to spiritual shame." *Shame and Grace—Healing the Shame We Don't Deserve* (San Francisco: Harper and Row, 1993), p. 42

89. I have written in greater depth about recovery from shame in *Self Care: A Theology of Personal Empowerment and Spiritual Healing* (Wheaton: Victor Books and Grand Rapids: Baker Books, 1995), Chapter Seven: "Shame: Letting of Emotional Self-Abuse," pp. 144-165.

90. Robert Bellah, et al. *Habits of the Heart—Individualism and Commitment in American Life* (Berkeley: University of California Press,1985), p. 153

91. The Christian psychologist, Craig Ellison, offers a definition that includes the elements of self concept and implies positive self worth by suggesting that self-esteem results from a comparison between the perceived self and the ideal self. "The most commonly accepted analysis of self-esteem sees it as the result of comparisons between one's perceived self, which combines both the assessments of others and one's private perceptions, and the ideal self, which is both how one feels one would like to be and how one feels one ought to be." Craig Ellison, *Your Better Self: Christianity, Psychology, and Self-Esteem* (New York: Harper and Row,

1983), p. 3.

92. Dr. Archibald Hart, Dean of the Graduate School of Psychology at Fuller Theological Seminary suggests that both low and high self-esteem may be unhealthy. "It is sufficient to stop hating yourself," he concludes. "For me a healthy attitude of the self toward the self is the absence of self-hate." *Unlocking the Mystery of your Emotions* (Dallas: Word Publishing, 1979, 1989), p. 94

93. As a case study in recovery from shame and self condemnation, I wrote the book, *The Gospel According to Judas: Is There a Limit to God's Forgiveness?* (Colorado Springs: NavPress, 1991, 1994). For some suggested steps toward recovery, see pp. 137ff

94. For practical help in stopping self-shaming habits and deflecting the shaming words and actions of others, I recommend the book by Curtis Levang, *The Adam and Eve Complex--Freedom from the Shame that Can Separate you from God, Others, and Yourself* (Minneapolis: SelfCare Books, 1992), especially pp. 79-87.

95. Martin Buber, the Jewish philosopher most remembered for his classic treatise on the nature of the self as personal and relational wrote: "The You encounters me by grace--it cannot be found by seeking. . . .The basic word I-You can be spoken only with one's whole being. The concentration and fusion into a whole being can never be accomplished by me, can never be accomplished without me. I require a You to become: being I, I say you." *I and Thou*, tr. by Walter Kaufman (Edinburgh: T. & T. Clark, 1979), p. 62.

96. George Gallop . "Buddhist Practices Make Inroads in the US," *The Christian Science Monitor* (November 3, 1997), p. 9.

97. For example: *Soul Care: Deliverance and Renewal Through the Christian Life*, by Kenneth Collins (1995), *The Secret Life of the Soul*, by Keith Miller (1997), *Living Life from the Soul: How a Man Unleashes God's Power from the Inside Out*, by Robert C. Crosby (1997) and, *Satisfy Your Soul: Restoring the Heart of Christian Spirituality*, by Bruce Demarest (1999).

98. See, *Satisfy Your Soul: Restoring the Heart of Christian Spirituality*, Bruce Demarest (Colorado Springs: NavPress, 1999), pp. 51ff.

99. Douglas Webster. Soulcraft: *How God Shapes us Through Relationships* (Downers Grove: InterVarsity Press, 1999), pp. 10; 209.

100. Edna St. Vincent Millay, "Wine from these Grapes," sonnet 10, in *Collected Poems*, ed. Norman Millay (New York: Harper and Row, 1956), p. 710.

101. Keith Miller. *The Secret Life of the Soul*, (Nashville: Broadman and Holman, Publishers, 1997),

102. Scott Peck, *Denial of the Soul*, p. 153.

103. *The Seat of the Soul*, p. 42.

104. Dylan Thomas, *The Poems of Dylan Thomas* (New York: New Directions Publications, 1971), p. 208.

105. Thomas Wolfe, *Look Homeward Angel!* (New York: Charles Scribner's Sons, 1930, Frontispiece).

106. *Denial of the Soul*, p. 153.

107. *Denial of the Soul*, p. 154.

108. I have discussed the phenomena associated with 'near death' experiences in my book, *Theology, Death and Dying*, "Christian Hope and Life Beyond Death," pp. 104-123 (Oxford: Basil Blackwell, 1986).

109. Murray J. Harris. *Raised Immortal--Resurrection and Immortality in the New Testament* (Grand Rapids: Eerdmans Publishing Company, 1983), pp. 140; 237. See also his later book, *From the Grave to Glory: Resurrection in the New Testament* (Grand Rapids: Zondervan, 1990), pp. 210ff; and, L. Cerfaaux. *The Christian in the Theology of St. Paul* (London: Chapman, 1967), pp. 190ff.

110. *The Seat of the Soul*, p. 86.

111. For example, see, John W. Cooper, *Body, Soul, & Life Everlasting--Biblical Anthropology and the Monism-Dualism Debate* (Grand Rapids: Eerdmans Publishing Company, 1989), p. 209. I have discussed this further in my book, *On Being Human: Essays in Theological Anthropology* (Grand Rapids: Eerdmans Publishing Company, 1982), p. 213.

112. Helmut Thielicke, *Living with Death* (Grand Rapids: Eerdmans, 1983), pp. 176-7.

113. Thomas F. Torrance, *Space, Time and Resurrection* (Grand Rapids: Eerdmans, 1976), p. 102,

Endnotes

114. Sister Madeleva, *The Four Last Things—Collected Poems* (New York: The Macmillan Company, 1959), p. 6.

www.ingramcontent.com/pod-product-compliance
Lightning Source LLC
Chambersburg PA
CBHW072152160426
43197CB00012B/2347